W9-DBW-727

THE AMERICAN TEENAGER

The American Teenager

EXAMINING POP CULTURE

KATE BURNS, Book Editor

Daniel Leone, President
Bonnie Szumski, Publisher
Scott Barbour, Managing Editor

GREENHAVEN
PRESS ®

THOMSON

GALE

San Diego • Detroit • New York • San Francisco • Cleveland
New Haven, Conn. • Waterville, Maine • London • Munich

LIBRARY OF CONGRESS CATALOGING-IN-PUBLICATION DATA

The American Teenager / Kate Burns, book editor.
    p. cm.—(Examining pop culture series)
Includes bibliographical references and index.
ISBN 0-7377-1467-0 (pbk. : alk. paper) — ISBN 0-7377-1466-2 (lib. : alk. paper)
    1. Teenagers—United States. 2. Teenagers—United States—Social conditions.
3. Mass media and teenagers—United States. 4. Teenage consumers—United
States. 5. Popular culture—United States. I. Burns, Kate. II. Series.
HQ796 .A674 2003
305.235'0973—dc21   2002035392

Printed in the United States of America

CONTENTS

Chapter 1: The Teenager in History

   Cynthia Lightfoot
   Adolescence is often associated with taking risks.
   Since the ancient Greeks, many have debated
   whether such youthful behavior should be encouraged or discouraged. This issue has produced a history of ambivalence about teenage experimentation,
   autonomy, and identity development.

   Grace Palladino
   The inauguration of a thriving teen culture in mid–
   twentieth century America had as much to do with
   big business as with teenagers themselves. In order
   to market their products, advertisers tapped into
   popular culture and promoted adolescence as a distinct stage of life separate from both childhood and
   adulthood.

   Aniko Bodroghkozy
   Children born during the post–World War II baby
   boom were the first generation to grow up with
   television sets in their homes. This new medium
   influenced profound political, social, and cultural
   changes in American life for young people coming
   of age in the 1950s and 1960s.

Chapter 2: Youth Cultures

Chapter 3: Teen Consumers

Chapter 4: Sex, Drugs, Violence, and Moral Panic

Chapter 5: Representing Teenagers in Pop Culture

POPULAR CULTURE IS THE COMMON SET OF ARTS, entertainments, customs, beliefs, and values shared by large segments of society. Russel B. Nye, one of the founders of the study of popular culture, wrote that "not until the appearance of mass society in the eighteenth century could popular culture, as one now uses the term, be said to exist." According to Nye, the Industrial Revolution and the rise of democracy in the eighteenth and nineteenth centuries led to increased urbanization and the emergence of a powerful middle class. In nineteenth-century Europe and North America, these trends created audiences for the popular arts that were larger, more concentrated, and more well off than at any point in history. As a result, more people shared a common culture than ever before.

The technological advancements of the twentieth century vastly accelerated the spread of popular culture. With each new advance in mass communication—motion pictures, radio, television, and the Internet—popular culture has become an increasingly pervasive aspect of everyday life.

Popular entertainment—in the form of movies, television, theater, music recordings and concerts, books, magazines, sporting events, video games, restaurants, casinos, theme parks, and other attractions—is one very recognizable aspect of popular culture. In his 1999 book *The Entertainment Economy: How Mega-Media Forces Are Transforming Our Lives*, Michael J. Wolf argues that entertainment is becoming the dominant feature of American society: "In choosing where we buy French fries, how we relate to political candidates, what airline we want to fly, what pajamas we choose for our kids, and which mall we want to buy them in, entertainment is increasingly influencing every one of those choices. . . . Multiply that by the billions of choices that, collectively, all of us make each day and you have a portrait of a society in which entertainment is one of its leading institutions."

It is partly this pervasive quality of popular culture that makes it worthy of study. James Combs, the author of *Polpop: Politics and Popular Culture in America*, explains that examining popular culture is important because it can shape people's attitudes and beliefs:

> Popular culture is so much a part of our lives that we cannot deny its developmental powers. . . . Like formal education or family rearing, popular culture is part of our "learning environment.". . . Though our pop culture education is informal—we usually do not attend to pop culture for its "educational" value—it nevertheless provides us with information and images upon which we develop our opinions and attitudes. We would not be what we are, nor would our society be quite the same, without the impact of popular culture.

Examining popular culture is also important because popular movies, music, fads, and the like often reflect popular opinions and attitudes. Christopher D. Geist and Jack Nachbar explain in *The Popular Culture Reader*, "the popular arts provide a gauge by which we can learn what Americans are thinking, their fears, fantasies, dreams, and dominant mythologies. The popular arts reflect the values of the multitude."

This two-way relationship between popular culture and society is evident in many modern discussions of popular culture. Does the glorification of guns by many rap artists, for example, merely reflect the realities of inner-city life, or does it also contribute to the problem of gun violence? Such questions also arise in discussions of the popular culture of the past. Did the Vietnam protest music of the late 1960s and early 1970s, for instance, simply reflect popular antiwar sentiments, or did it help turn public opinion against the war? Examining such questions is an important part of understanding history.

Greenhaven Press's *Examining Pop Culture* series provides students with the resources to begin exploring these questions. Each volume in the series focuses on a particular aspect of popular culture, with topics as varied as popular culture itself. Books in the series may focus on a particular genre, such as *Rap and Hip Hop*, while others may cover a specific medium, such as *Computers and the Internet*. Volumes such as *Body Piercing and Tattoos* have their focus on recent trends in popular culture, while titles like *Americans' Views About War* have a broader historical scope.

In each volume, an introductory essay provides a general

overview of the topic. The selections that follow offer a survey of critical thought about the subject. The readings in *Americans' Views About War*, for example, are arranged chronologically: Essays explore how popular films, songs, television programs, and even comic books both reflected and shaped public opinion about American wars from World War I through Vietnam. The essays in *Violence in Film and Television*, on the other hand, take a more varied approach: Some provide historical background, while others examine specific genres of violent film, such as horror, and still others discuss the current controversy surrounding the issue.

Each book in the series contains a comprehensive index to help readers quickly locate material of interest. Perhaps most importantly, each volume has an annotated bibliography to aid interested students in conducting further research on the topic. In today's culture, what is "popular" changes rapidly from year to year and even month to month. Those who study popular culture must constantly struggle to keep up. The volumes in Greenhaven's *Examining Pop Culture* series are intended to introduce readers to the major themes and issues associated with each topic, so they can begin examining for themselves what impact popular culture has on their own lives.

THE AMERICAN TEENAGER HAS BEEN A SOURCE of fascination since the mid–twentieth century. The population surge after World War II resulted in an explosion of teenagers by the 1960s, and young people could not be ignored. This generation inherited the name "baby boomers," describing the largest group of teens ever to hit the United States up to that time. Since then, America crowns each new generation with a similar buzz term, and social commentators offer formulas to capture the essence of each teen set. Baby boomers were said to be action oriented, skeptical of authority, and experimental. They ushered in a sexual revolution, danced to rock and roll, and led a massive protest movement against the Vietnam War. Following the boomers came "Generation X," usually described in contrast to their predecessors. The media characterized this group as the "Me" generation, the self-absorbed and disillusioned victims of an accelerated commodity culture.

The New Breed

Succeeding them, the newest generation has many names already. Some people link the new teens to a second baby boom, calling them "echo boomers." Others say that what follows Generation X is "Generation Y." Still others mark this generation as the first to grow up online, calling them the "digital" generation, "Generation Wired" or "Generation IM" (for "instant message"). Seen as equally different from the baby boomers as they are from the Xers, these "millennials" (who have crossed into the twenty-first century) will end up 77 million strong—greater in number than any other teenage population. Many agree, as *Fortune* magazine proclaims, "these kids are a new breed."[1]

Just how the new teenagers are unique is still debated. Critics of the American obsession to classify and label each generation point out that it is impossible to account for the diversity of so many individuals. They question why people become fixated with categorizing teenagers at the risk of pigeonholing them into meaningless divisions. But one extremely powerful segment of society is willing to take that chance. Big business channels copious time and money into discovering categories that accurately describe teen tastes, desires, and group identities. Their efforts are meaningful—at least to their bottom-line goal: profit. They are in a rush to understand teenagers in order to launch successful mass-marketing campaigns. Their hope is to produce unprecedented profits in the short term and, moreover, to win the long-term loyalty of lifetime customers when teens age into successive stages of adulthood. More than any other venue, popular culture tells big business "where it's at" when it comes to teens. Businesses take the time to keep up with popular culture because they know that teen numbers are growing at a faster rate than the overall U.S. population. The sheer size of the teenage population is an important part of what makes it the hottest marketing demographic since the baby boomer generation.

Teen Spending Power

The size of teen piggy banks is an equally important factor. *Entrepreneur* magazine recently quipped, "Teens are sooo money!"[2] encouraging businesses to cash in on the $155 billion market. In addition to spending their own money, teens influence family spending decisions more than ever before. Retailers have recently realized that teenagers "often have a decisive say in the purchase of big-ticket [family] items,"[3] according to *Marketing* magazine. The research firm Imagination Youth Marketing estimates that 80 percent of parents consult teens before selecting a family vacation, 64 percent before selecting a computer, and 25 percent before selecting a car.[4] Changes in family structure have increased teen influence over the years. Single, divorced, or two-paycheck parents are becoming the norm for many children growing up in the twenty-first century. Adults, often plagued with multiple responsibilities inside and outside the home, delegate more household tasks to teenagers. As early as 1990, the marketing firm Impact Resources reported that "no adult is home during the day in 70% of households, which means a sizable part of the $40 billion spent on groceries and other household items passes through teens' hands."[5] As the family unit has changed, so have the roles of family members.

Furthermore, teenagers are earning their own disposable incomes. At the end of the 1990s, 41 percent of sixteen- to eighteen-year-olds worked full- or part-time. When babysitting and other unrecorded jobs were included in the equation, three-quarters of all teens earned some money from working.[6] Add in allowances and gifts and it is clear that teen wallets and purses are getting fatter every year. What persuades teens to part with cash from their own pockets and from the family cookie jar? According to many marketing surveys, teenagers like nothing better than spending their earnings on clothes, entertainment, and fast food. Brand names and fashionable merchandise have become central to adolescent identity for many young people. When asked about teen life in the new millennium, an eleventh-grader explained to *Maclean's* magazine, "It's all about pop culture. And pop culture is about buying."[7]

This stronger-than-ever link between teen popular culture and consumption means that retailers who tended to ignore teenagers after the baby boom era are now begging teens to explain what they want in a product. Since teen tastes change at a fast pace, new methods are being explored to track youth trends. To avoid the slow process of publishing reports in print, Lreport.com marketing company canvasses a network of young consumers in six U.S. cities and sends updates on trends to clients via the Internet. "The pace of changing trends has become so fast," says general manager Maria Vrachnos, that "the time to collect the data and get it onto paper can take too long and our clients don't want to miss trends—they want to catch them in their infancy. . . . Books can be very cumbersome. We're not doing the hard copies anymore."[8] Also avoiding the slow process of publishing in print, the research company Informer interviews a group of teenagers every month and compiles CD-ROMs for quick review. Another firm videotapes girls over a twenty-five-hour period, listening in on conversations and observing every activity in school, at home, or out with friends. The strategy is to get a deeper understanding of teen lifestyles in order to mesh teen priorities with advertising messages. On the one hand, this rising interest in youth culture can be seen as a refreshing form of teen power. On the other hand, equating teenagers' importance with their ability to spend money is disconcerting to those who worry about teen exploitation.

Teen Power Versus Teen Exploitation

This concern is at the heart of the controversy over whether teenagers drive the market or whether industries manipulate teenagers. The debate gets especially contentious when it comes to tobacco and alcohol products. If teens look to popular culture for clues about what is cool, a lot of what they are seeing is smoking and drinking. Parents, teachers, and other advocates of teen welfare ask whether young consumers have the ability to critically evaluate advertising that glamorizes risky behavior. Teens may be encouraged to experiment with products that can lead to health problems, addiction, and even death. The American Cancer Society reports that 90 percent of new smokers are children and teenagers; over three thousand adolescents smoke their first cigarette each day in the United States. One-third of these new smokers will someday die of tobacco-related diseases according to usual addiction rates.

Tobacco and alcohol advertisers repeatedly deny that they market to teens. Many watchdog groups think otherwise. A recent study for the National Safety Council on Teen Alcohol Use notes that a large alcohol producer was one of the major advertisers during televised coverage of Indiana's Sweet 16 high school basketball play-offs. Thousands of teen viewers tuned in. Likewise, the publication *Current Health 2* reports that "alcohol producers sponsor many events aimed at teens: sports, contests, tasting parties, and rock bands. They give away T-shirts, mugs, hats, posters, toys, stuffed animals, and other things that appeal to teens."[9] Evidence like this adds fuel to the concern that teenagers may be vulnerable to underhanded advertising tactics.

Yet many who study consumer trends claim that the new teenager is better at seeing through slick ad campaigns than most adults. One common quality attributed to the new generation is that they are *very* savvy customers. The message from research firms is a warning to advertisers: Do not talk down to today's teens! According to New York–based Zandi Group, a marketing research firm that polls one thousand teens monthly, "teens are smarter shoppers than boomers were at the same age. . . . They have been exposed to so much through television and it has made them more aware and less quick to trust."[10]

Maclean's magazine echoes that sentiment, saying that teens "consider themselves immune to the tricks of the advertising trade. Bombarded from birth, they know they are being pitched and are suspicious. They recognize their own power."[11]

The Fragmented Generation

Inundated with more advertising than any previous generation, teens have had ample opportunities to test advertising promises against what a product really delivers. They also tend to understand how important their dollars are to industries that want their loyalty. Many believe that this sense of entitlement makes them more likely to assert their exacting demands. With more products to choose from that are developed specifically to please teens, they are less likely to buy as a single mass set of consumers. "Increasingly young people are fragmented and elusive," says Kristine Burnett, editor of Informer marketing research reports. "They live in an accelerated culture where advertisers are struggling to keep up. The moment you think you have a grip on youth culture is the moment you are furthest from understanding it."[12] Due to their consumer sophistication and diversity, many advertisers find this generation particularly difficult to pin down.

Accordingly, rather than approach the new generation as a single unit, big business has learned to embrace teenage diversity. In order to attract teen dollars, more advertisers are mirroring their target demographic. When asked in a recent survey for the single most important marketing trend, 250 marketing vice presidents chose "fragmentation." In other words, the old strategy of "repeat[ing] a brand name like a mantra on network television" can no longer guarantee loyal teen customers since "there are too many other media and leisure alternatives competing for the attention of jaded consumers."[13] New strategies recognize that teenagers are made up of many different subgroups. Advertisers divide the larger demographic into smaller target categories to see if they can capture the variety of teen styles more accurately.

One division centers on age groups. Due to the faster pace of growing up these days, the "cool factor" starts at a younger age. To advertisers, even eight- and nine-year-olds are considered part of the larger teenage demographic. However, they recognize that young teens may have markedly different preferences than older teens and divide the target audiences correspondingly. In ad-speak, nine- to fourteen-year-olds are "tweens" and fifteen- to nineteen-year-olds are "teens."[14] *Advertising Age* magazine explains, "Tween consumers are not just older children or preteens but a well-defined market segment with its own tastes and desires."[15] Marketing research says that tweens are more refined consumers than younger kids, yet not as suspicious of advertising as older teens. Tweens tend to make their money from odd jobs and allowances; teens are more likely to have regular employment. Although it is estimated that tweens spend $14 billion a year, some retailers still are reluctant to sell directly to them. For example, some cosmetic companies are skittish about pushing full-blown makeup lines to young girls who already feel enough pressure to grow up fast. This reluctance will fade, predicts tween marketing expert Tim Coffey, as industries "wake up to the fact that this is a huge market."[16]

Advertising campaigns also divide the teenage demographic to account for differences other than age. Some clothing retailers focus their pitch on trendsetting teens, others appeal to those more comfortable in the mainstream. The Christian youth products industry is growing rapidly with separate lines of music, videos, comics, and magazines.[17] Changes in gender expectations have companies like Nike tapping into girl-power vogue. Tracking new fads and identities in youth culture can become complicated. Teens today are more likely to cross conventional boundary lines of race, ethnicity, and class to participate in popular culture trends. New technologies facilitate global interaction among teens from many different countries. *Maclean's* magazine reports, "in the 1970s and 1980s, adolescents could pretty much be divided into jocks, rockers, and preps. Now . . . there are at least a dozen teen 'tribes' defined by their fashion, music and magazines."[18] Keeping up with teenagers is a challenging task. As marketing consultant Paul McGowan warns, "treat the youth market as one market and you will become bland and young people will recognize that."[19]

Tricks of the Advertising Trade

Advertisers have come up with several new strategies to reach this fragmented generation. Most agree that the old tactic of relying on network TV ads is out of date. The majority of teenagers today know their way around a variety of new technologies. Television is only one component of their multimedia arsenal—mobile phones, pagers, and the Internet also play a major part in their lives.[20] *Entrepreneur* magazine reports that "teens use the Net more than ever before to chat, download music—they're even breaking up [their relationships] online."[21] Of the 13 million teens online in 2001, 74 percent used instant messaging, compared to only 44 percent of adults. With their greater access to a variety of media, teens tend to utilize several formats at once. "[Teens] are multitasking—they're instant messaging, watching TV, listening to the radio and flipping through a magazine at the same time,"[22] says Larry Adams, account director of a youth Web marketing firm. This has inspired marketing strategies to keep up with teenage multitasking.

One advertising technique is called "cross-referencing." In this endeavor, several companies join forces to promote their products together. Lindsay Meredith, professor of marketing at Simon Fraser University, explains cross-referencing as an unprecedented "interlocking of movies with sports, TV and toys that previous generations never experienced. The movie sells the toy and the toy sells the movie. That means it's not as easy for a parent to say no."[23] When fast-food restaurants sell movie action figures with hamburgers and fries, they are engaging in cross-referencing advertising. A related technique is for a single brand to send its message across many venues. As Brad Adgate of Horizon Media says, "reaching the non-adult sector is a multi-tiered process."[24] Using this technique, a brand may put commercials on network TV, but it also will advertise via cable TV, the Internet, syndication, print, movies, radio, and sponsorship activities. Both of these concentrated selling techniques are designed to promote an acute awareness of brand names.

Other strategies include spin-offs and designer retail outlets. Spin-offs tap into a teen's desire to be perceived as an adult. In this approach, products already familiar as adult brands generate separate lines just for teens. From 1999 to 2000, for example, three new spin-off teen magazines appeared on newsstands. *Cosmopolitan* created *CosmoGIRL!*,

Men's Health created *MH-18*, and *Vogue* created *Teen Vogue*. This piggybacking of new products on already successful adult products reduces the risk of failure. In contrast to marketing to wanna-be adults, designer retail shops aim to make teens feel special as young customers. Many retailers upgrade their teen departments by adorning walls with screens showing music videos. Some go much further. Skinmarket, a line of fashion accessories for teen girls, designs its stores to mimic a girl's bedroom. Founder Tony Hirsch explains, "they are decorated with funky colors and contain makeup-application stations and seating areas where the girls can gossip, read magazines or listen to music for as long as they want—without buying a thing."[25] Skinmarket also hosts parties and staffs the stores with girls the same age as customers. The result is a large following of comfortable loiterers who, it is hoped, will become regular impulse buyers.

Corporate advertisers are also moving into classrooms. In return for the right to sell their products while school is in session, businesses offer equipment like TVs, computers, and other educational items. By producing "sponsored educational materials," companies advertise while they teach students about credit cards, the environment, or nutrition. Schools with ever decreasing budgets find the corporate "gifts" hard to turn down. Channel One, a twelve-minute news program offered to schools by Whittle Communications, requires schools to show two minutes of commercials during class time. The payoff is free TVs, VCRs, and satellite dishes to broadcast the program. By 1993, the show aired in over ten thousand schools, reaching about 8 million students. This was twice the audience of the hottest concurrent teen-oriented program on commercial TV, *Beverly Hills 90210*.

Is Youth Culture *Only* About Buying?

Some experts say that the marriage between teen popular culture and rabid consumerism will continue to thrive. With the help of new technologies, American teen culture is blending with a global teen culture. UNICEF reported that half the world's population was under the age of twenty years in 2002. *Whole Earth Review* magazine states that "there is a Global Teenager emerging, global both in proportion and in perspective," and predicts that "billions of teenagers will listen to the same music, watch the same movies, wear the same clothes, and perhaps study the same things in school."[26]

Other experts forecast an inevitable backlash against the trend toward blatant materialism. "There is not a well-expressed oppositional culture among today's youth," says Sean Saraq of the trend-watching company Youth Culture Inc., "but anticonsumerism is growing and it will find a voice."[27] Teens could be suffering from advertising fatigue. As one young man professed to *Maclean's* magazine, "I don't want my life to revolve around buying and selling. There should be some safe haven from advertising. You have to sometimes see the sky between the billboards."[28]

Examining the American Teenager in Popular Culture

The relationship between consumerism and teen culture will continue to generate important discussions about priorities and principles in American society. As new generations bring their cultural styles to the mix, they will inspire additional questions to be explored. There is much to learn from the segment of society positioned between children and adults.

The essays in *Examining Pop Culture: The American Teenager* investigate a variety of topics related to youth culture and the popular media. It is hoped that this collection will stimulate critical thinking about the complex social issues that circulate in controversies about teenagers and popular culture, issues that sometimes influence political agendas and public policy. By examining the American teenager and popular culture, readers can explore a subject that has enduring national and global implications.

Notes

1. Shawn Tully, "The Universal Teenager," *Fortune*, April 4, 1994, pp. 14–16.

2. Nichole L. Torres, "Teen Green," *Entrepreneur*, December 2001, pp. 26+.

3. Andy Fry, "Brands Cash in by Targeting Tweens," *Marketing*, October 12, 2000, p. 39.

4. Quoted in Pam Withers, "Move Over, Boomers," *BC Business*, June 1998, pp. 28+.

5. Quoted in Debra Goldman, "The New Consumer," *Adweek's Marketing Week*, September 17, 1990, pp. 25+.

6. Nina Munk, "Girl Power!" *Fortune*, December 8, 1997, pp. 133+.

7. Quoted in *Maclean's*, "How Teens Got the Power," March 22, 1999, pp. 42–49.

8. Quoted in Rusty Williamson, "L Report Goes Online to Track Teens," *WWD*, December 28, 2000, p. 9.

9. Judy Monroe, "Alcohol and Ads: What Effect Do They Have on You?" *Current Health 2*, November 1994, pp. 24+.

10. Quoted in Mary Nelson, "Teen Spirit," *Sporting Goods Business*, July 1995, pp. 92+.

11. *Maclean's*, "How Teens Got the Power," pp. 42–49.

12. Quoted in Richard Cook, "Understanding Teenagers and TV," *Campaign*, September 5, 1997, p. 38.

13. Goldman, "The New Consumer," pp. 25+.

14. *Maclean's*, "How Teens Got the Power," pp. 42–49.

15. Chantal Tode, "Evolution of Tweens' Tastes Keeps Retailers on Their Toes," *Advertising Age*, February 12, 2001, pp. S6+.

16. Quoted in Tode, "Evolution of Tweens' Tastes," pp. S6+.

17. Heather Hendershot, "Shake, Rattle & Roll: Production and Consumption of Fundamentalist Youth Culture," *Afterimage*, February/March 1995, pp. 19+.

18. *Maclean's*, "How Teens Got the Power," pp. 42–49.

19. Quoted in Elaine Cavanagh, "Wise Up or Ship Out," *In-Store Marketing*, August 2000, p. 28.

20. Robert Gray, "Hit a Moving Target," *Marketing*, November 16, 2000, p. 45.

21. Nichole L. Torres, "Teen Green," *Entrepreneur*, December 2001, pp. 26+.

22. Quoted in Torres, "Teen Green," pp. 26+.

23. Quoted in *Maclean's*, "How Teens Got the Power," pp. 42–49.

24. Quoted in Marc Berman, "Teen Angles," *Brandweek*, May 31, 1999, pp. 24+.

25. Quoted in Norinne de Gal, "Retailers Turn Stores into Hangouts to Attract Teens," *Los Angeles Business Journal*, July 17, 2000, p. 11.

26. Quoted in UNICEF, *Sustainability Student Action Kit*, October 12, 2002. www.globalvision.org/sustainability/audience.html.

27. Quoted in *Maclean's*, "How Teens Got the Power," pp. 42–49.

28. Quoted in *Maclean's*, "How Teens Got the Power," pp. 42–49.

1

EXAMINING POP CULTURE

The Teenager in History

Risk-Taking: The Image of Teens in Popular Culture

Cynthia Lightfoot

Most studies about adolescent life and teen culture have been dominated by the viewpoint of adults. Cynthia Lightfoot wanted to change that trend when she wrote *The Culture of Adolescent Risk-Taking* in 1997. To enhance her research, she interviewed over forty teenagers to collect their ideas about taking risks during the teen years. The conclusion she presents is that risk-taking is a meaningful activity from the vantage point of teenagers. To contextualize her study, Lightfoot draws from anthropology, psychology, literature, and popular culture to interpret how adolescent risk involvement has been represented historically. This excerpt from her book provides an overview of our cultural ambivalence toward the subject. On the one hand, we tend to romanticize young adventurers and see their exploits as rites of passage. On the other hand, we condemn risk-taking as dangerous—to teenagers themselves and to the moral foundation of their communities. Lightfoot maintains that we need to acknowledge the mixed messages in order to better understand the relevance of risk involvement to teen cultural identity.

A TEENAGER TOLD ME THAT "IF YOU PLOD ALONG and do the same boring old thing your whole damn life you'll

■

die a boring old fart." This was to justify his risk involvement, which included sneaking out of the house in the middle of the night to share a joint with friends, skipping school to drop acid at the beach, and picking fights with rednecks and frat boys. My reaction was probably typical—good humor riding the tail of astonishment—and I suppose that the historical stamina of our interest in adolescent risk-taking owes some debt to the double meanings that we attach to these behaviors. On the one hand, many have gained notoriety as "social problems," manifestations of an insidious pathology overtaking the body of contemporary society. The sentiment is hardly overstated in a time during which teen violence and homicides roil suburbs and inner cities alike, and HIV moves rapidly and perniciously among the teen population. Yet we romanticize youth's disposition for mischief with equal enthusiasm. Our literature and folklore make heroes of young adventurers and invite nostalgic reflection on a time in our lives when taking risks created windows of possibility and was seen to test our mettle, if not our maturity. Throughout history we have brought these behaviors into focus with two apparently incompatible lenses. One provides a view of risk-taking as trouble, the other as opportunity.

Risk-Taking as Trouble

Popular interest in adolescents' risk involvement began even before the adults in their lives determined that they were coherent enough as a group to deserve a name, that is, before *adolescence* became a household word. American psychologist G. Stanley Hall (1904) popularized this label for those between childhood and maturity, but its widespread acceptance had as much to do with larger social and economic processes as it did with the nature of teenagers themselves. The most significant was the need for a formally educated citizenry created by the industrial revolution. As education for children became more systematized in the late 1800s and early 1900s, older children became more visible. We devised special school curricula for them, and beyond that, engineered social environments in which they spent large amounts of time hanging out with same-age peers. The adolescent peer group, in many ways an adaptation to these economic and educational reforms, came to supplant the mixed-age social groups of years past.

It is interesting, and telling, that at the time our society began to take note of adolescents and their groups, the eyes of educators, philosophers, and scientists turned quickly to their misbehaviors. Large boys, in particular, attracted much attention. They were widely recognized as being high-spirited, reckless, difficult to control, overconfident, and inclined to drop out of school. Teachers were called upon to address the special problems presented by those of their pupils who were in that awkward place between childhood and adulthood.

Still, we can reach back to a time before "adolescence" became embodied in school curricula, youth organizations, and judicial systems, that is, before it became institutionalized, and find references to individuals with a foot on each side of whatever it means to be fully mature. Even here they are replete with warnings of impending disaster. Plato proposed a minimum drinking age because "fire should not be poured upon fire"; Aristotle made much of youthful passions, impulses, and feelings of omniscience; French philosopher Jean Jacques Rousseau compared the adolescent to a lion in season, distrustful of his keeper and ungovernable:

> As the roaring of the waves precedes the tempest, so the murmur of rising passions announces this tumultuous change: a suppressed excitement warns us of the approaching danger. A change of temper, frequent outbreaks of anger, a perpetual stirring of the mind, make the child almost ungovernable. He becomes deaf to the voice he used to obey: he is a lion in a fever: he distrusts his keeper and refuses to be controlled.

These vivid and often violent images of youth also color the pages of English literature from the Middle Ages to the present. Chaucer, Shakespeare, Milton, Wordsworth—all present a vision of youth as characteristically excessive, passionate, proud, and sensual, and contrast it with the clear-eyed sobriety of adulthood. Heightened affectivity is the primary culprit. It stands accused of inclining youth toward adventures in love and war (Chaucer's *Canterbury Tales*), and underlies the first classic tale of teen suicide (Shakespeare's *Romeo and Juliet*). For Chaucer it disrupts normal functioning, sometimes to the point of inducing bad health: "So hot he loved that at nighttime / He slept no more than does a nightingale."

Shakespeare is expert at such depictions, both tragic, as in *Romeo and Juliet*, and comic, as in *The Merchant of Venice*, in which Portia disguises herself as a young man and explains that she must

> . . . speak of frays
> Like a fine bragging youth, and tell quaint lies,
> How honorable ladies sought my love,
> Which I denying, they fell sick and died—
> (act 3, scene 4, lines 70–73)

Youths lose more than sleep and health to unbridled emotion. Reason is another victim, and sensibility, discretion, good taste, even character. Animal metaphors abound; thus, Shakespeare was moved to record that "for young hot colts being raged, do rage the more" (*Richard II*, act 2, scene 1, line 70). These images penetrate deeply into the literary and philosophical canons of Western thought, and throughout we find expressions of concern about youth's inclinations for getting into trouble, and advice on how to steer them away from it.

Controlling Trouble

Clothed in the language and methods of modern science, this *risk-taking-as-trouble* orientation has organized a massive effort aimed at identifying the epidemiological, sociological, and developmental correlates of adolescents' risk behaviors. Over the longer haul, and in the tradition of the empiricist approach that frames this research, the goal is to pinpoint specific causes so that risk involvement can be predicted and controlled. It is well intended: Our children are coming of age in an era gripped by unparalleled teen pregnancy, drug addiction, suicide, and homicide. Beyond these more obvious consequences, their risks are attended by school dropout, welfare dependency, and incarceration. The desire to locate antecedent conditions is coupled tightly with a felt need to contain pressing social problems that are destroying the families, neighborhoods, and lives of youth.

Although this orientation has surely held the larger measure of our attentions, one can also identify a different point of view. This one, grounded more securely in developmental theory, and closer to the *risk-taking-as-opportunity* view, has it that adolescent problem behaviors are demonstrative of normative developmental concerns and processes. Thus conceived, risk-taking is as bound to issues of experimentation, autonomy, and identity development as it is to rebellion, trouble-making, and mischief. . . .

Risk-Taking as Opportunity

As with the risk-taking-as-trouble orientation, the risk-taking-as-opportunity perspective also has roots in antiquity. In classical times, risks and adventures were construed as ordeals, tests of valor, virtue, strength, fidelity, and so forth, that were to be met and endured. Although this view dominated early European literature, a new vision of the hero emerged during the second half of the 18th century. The modern hero is one who takes on shape and character in consequence of risks and adventures; the modern hero *develops*. Remarkable events are not encountered by simple happenstance, but actively sought for their capacity to challenge and educate. It seems, then, that risks were not *taken*, exactly, until fairly recently. . . . I mean only to draw out the two cultural–historical casts responsible for our conflicted and ambivalent understanding of the adventures and misadventures of youth. U.S. philosopher John Dewey brings them into sharper relief when he describes our usual metric for the "goodness" of children as "the amount of trouble they make for grownups, which means of course the amount they deviate from adult habits and expectations. Yet by way of expiation we envy children their love of new experiences, their intentness in extracting the last drop of significance from each situation, their vital seriousness in things that to us are outworn."

By Dewey's reading, the happier moments of children's exploration and study are just as lively and significant as those that are querulous and potentially hurtful. American social reformer Jane Addams (1910) argued that the latter often overshadow the former, and obscure their common connections. At the turn of the century, she devoted a book to her experiences working with adolescents who arrived in America's industrial centers in unprecedented numbers. She wrote of their "quest for adventure" as a natural developmental period, and the source of their unflagging energy, enthusiasm, and zealous pursuit of novelty. But for many, newly arrived in a city illprepared to receive them, it was also their undoing: "The young people are overborne by their own undirected and misguided energies. A mere temperamental outbreak in a brief period of obstreperousness exposes a promising boy to arrest and imprisonment, an accidental combination of circumstances too complicated and overwhelming to be coped with by an immature mind, condemns a growing lad to a criminal career."

Science Studies Youth

Undirected, fevered, tempted, reckless: These are the essences of youth, the natural consequences of emotion unfurled and unchecked by higher mental functions. Surviving centuries of scrutiny by poets and philosophers, these essences remain unparched even by the hot lights of modern science. Indeed, psychological theories of adolescent development have from the beginning drawn breath from them. G. Stanley Hall (1904), author of the first comprehensive compendium of adolescent psychology (its title was nothing less than *Adolescence: Its Psychology and Its Relations to Physiology, Anthropology, Sociology, Sex, Crime, Religion, and Education*) adopted a biogenetic and recapitulationist posture. Believing that the development of each individual is a fast-forward replay of the evolution of the entire species—that ontogeny recapitulates phylogeny—Hall saw the restlessness, recklessness, and eagerness of adolescence as marking a turning point. In his view, it is only with the advent of adolescence that the individual for the first time breaks through the predetermined phyletic structure to act in ways that are truly individual, unique, and agentic: truly human, by Hall's lights. Adolescence heralds the end of the lockstep, phylogenetic sequence, and is accordingly a period of unprecedented flexibility and plasticity of thought, feeling, and behavior. Our best response, as parents, educators, or persons in other roles that minister to the well-being of children, is to give adolescents a loose rein and thereby enable their personal exploration and experimentation. Seeing in all of this an agenda for policy and education, Hall reasoned that because adolescents are by their very nature primed to be inspired, we ought to take steps to inspire them. History, he argued, ought to be the study of heroes, science the study of cosmic forces. Hall was the first to insist on a "moratorium" for youth, a time out from responsibility and obligation in order that they might explore in the freest possible manner the world and discover their places within it.

In modern scientific circles, the risk-taking-as-opportunity perspective can perhaps trace its lineage to Hall's grandiose beginnings. There is at least strong evidence of historical continuity: Hall's theory of moratoruim; Addams's report of youth's fitful "quest for adventure"; Erik Erikson's thesis of the adolescent "craving for locomotion:"

> The most widespread expression of the discontented search of youth is the craving for locomotion, whether expressed in a general "being on the go," "tearing after something," or "running around"; or in locomotion proper, as in vigorous work, in absorbing sports, in rapt dancing, in shiftless *Wanderschaft*, and in the employment and misuse of speedy animals and machines. But it also finds expression through participation in the movements of the day (whether the riots of a local commotion or the parades and campaigns of major ideological forces), if they only appeal to the need for feeling "moved" and for feeling essential in moving something along toward an open future.

Erikson's main thesis was that "locomotion" constitutes a form of excessive experimentation, of testing the limits of one's self, of exploring its multiple possibilities, especially its relations to society. All of this speaks to a search for "some durability in change," and for those who find it, a sense of identity interdependent with community and history. Thus, the concept of the "psychosocial moratorium" (popularized by Erikson, 1968), which continues to exert considerable force in modern identity development theory, is nothing less than a codification of the idea that adolescents engage in a period of experimentation from which they emerge with a foothold on who they will become. But whereas the risk-taking-as-trouble orientation has harnessed the energy of a generation of researchers bent on preventing adolescent risk-taking, the perspective put forth by Hall, Addams, and Erikson, and those of their ilk has been less seminal. Only recently have investigators considered the possibility that risk involvement may have positive consequences for psychosocial development. . . . Those sympathetic to this emerging point of view are making claims that pot smoking, wild driving, early sexual intimacy, and so forth, have strategic roles in achieving social status, demonstrating autonomy, and hedging boredom and anxiety. . . . In fact, in failing to provide resources that would promote alternative behaviors, the "Just Say No!" campaign dismisses the functional utility of adolescents' risks and guarantees that it will provide nothing more than ineffectual rhetoric with which to decorate car bumpers.

The Concept of Teenagers Created a Marketing Niche

Grace Palladino

The word "teenager" emerged into common language around the time of World War II to describe the high school experience of a new generation. Today, we take for granted the association of style, culture, and mind-set with the age group from thirteen to nineteen. In the 1940s, however, adolescence as a distinct stage in life was a new concept, and one that from its inception was tied intimately to marketplace strategy. With the encouragement of big business, teen culture became a burgeoning industry by the '50s. In the decades following, baby boomers took center stage while retail chains, magazines, TV networks, and manufacturing sought them as a valued independent niche. Changes in demographics, educational policy, and family expectations transformed the early version of the wholesome and still dependent ingenue of the '40s into the autonomous and often jaded young adult who demanded to govern his or her own actions, sexuality, and identity. Grace Palladino outlines the evolution of teen culture in this introduction to her often-cited book *Teenagers: An American History*. She also writes extensively about American labor history and is codirector of the Samuel Gompers Papers project at the University of Maryland, College Park.

■

"THEY'RE BACK!" THE COVER OF *BUSINESSWEEK* trumpeted in 1994. Better yet, there are going to be more of them than ever before, buying pizza, going to concerts, purchasing clothes, cosmetics, CDs, cars, and computer games. They sound like an advertiser's dream—a consumer group with the free time and disposable income to support an affluent life of leisure. Of course, that's exactly what they are—teenagers with more money to spend, more products to choose from, and enough influence in the marketplace to crowd out their baby-boomer parents. After a fifteen-year population decline from 1977 to 1992, teenagers are now riding the crest of a demographic wave that promises big business for years to come. And that almost guarantees them a prominent place in the public spotlight. For no matter what we profess to believe about teenagers and their vital importance to the future, we tend to value them most as consumers.

It's a role that seems oddly suited to their stage in life. "The teen years, after all, are a time of experiment," as *Business-Week* puts it. "Trying on new fashions, music, TV shows and movies, products, ideas and attitudes, is what being a teen is all about." Caught in the crosswinds of puberty and inexperience, they are notoriously obsessed with their complexions, their appearance, their social life—typical teenage problems that have spawned a thriving industry of advice givers, guidance counselors, orthodontists, dermatologists. Their legendary need to fit in with the crowd generates healthy profits for a host of businesses from clothing manufacturers to pop music producers—teenagers are almost driven to keep up with the latest products and styles, marketers point out. With a population of 25 million and counting (there should be almost 31 million teenagers by 2006, an all-time high), they constitute a red-hot consumer market worth $89 billion—almost ten times what the market was reportedly worth in 1957, when Elvis Presley was riding high.

That doesn't even begin to count the $200 billion their parents spend on them, either—a healthy figure in anyone's book. In fact, since parents are likely to be at their peak earning power by the time their children are in high school, they are considered a teenager's greatest financial asset. "Parents give teens what teens think of as necessities—a car, a computer, video games," market researchers report. But since teenagers choose the products themselves, companies are advised to court them directly with specialized products, services, and advertising campaigns. "Marketers ignore this group at their peril," a car manufacturer insists, since teenage shoppers are known in the business as "early adopters." Those who develop product loyalties when they are still young and impressionable will carry them through adulthood, marketers promise. And at that point they will have even more money to spend—a tantalizing prospect, given current population trends.

Birth of the Teenager

Crass exploitation? Perhaps. A disturbing sign of the times? Hardly. A new corruption of teenage life? Absolutely not. On the contrary, the *BusinessWeek* article is only the latest version of promotional material that has been circulating for decades. Ever since the word "teenager" first came into popular use around the time of the Second World War, the group has been linked to "buying power and influence," a heady combination that promised big business to postwar moviemakers, cosmetic firms, clothes manufacturers, and even grocery stores. At the time, the change was revolutionary—only a decade or so earlier, most teenage children had worked for a living. In fact some had been required to pay back the debts they had incurred in childhood before they were free to leave the family home! They, not their parents, were considered assets to be exploited for a family's good, and they usually had very little to say about this or any other family matter.

Now they were identified as high school students with the time and the inclination to shop for clothes, party goods, records. But in the 1940s retailers found this hard to believe at first. Since nobody knew whether teenagers actually had money to spend, they doubted their value in the marketplace. So fifty years ago promoters launched the idea that teenagers could be counted on to spend their parents' money—after all, they were the family members most likely to demand well-appointed recreation rooms, up-to-date cars, modern appliances, and the latest electronic equipment. And they apparently had no trouble at all getting what they wanted. Now that the war was over, promoters pointed out, parents were willing and able to "play Santa Claus 365 days a year." But if companies wanted a piece of this business, they added, they would have to speak directly to the kids themselves, a proposition that was controversial at the time. Teenagers were still considered children in society's eyes, and that meant they required guidance and protection in the marketplace.

Autonomous Consumers

Today those concerns are still raised periodically, but the market itself has settled the controversy. The concept of teenagers as an independent age group with its own interests, attitudes, and spending money is so ingrained that high school students rule their own commercial space—retail chains like Urban Outfitters and the Gap vie for their business; magazine publishers offer *Seventeen, Sassy, YM,* and *Teen* (among others); and television networks like Fox and MTV program with their demographics in mind. Newspapers from the *Staten Island Advance* to the *Santa Fe New Mexican* feature weekly sections devoted to teenage issues that range from roller blading to body piercing, from prom clothes to mosh pits, to what's hot and what's not. Manufacturers recognize their buying power with specialized lines of "teen spirit" products or makeup specifically formulated to combat teenage "zits." Indeed, as far as marketers are concerned, teenagers inhabit their own leisure world, one that is dominated by movies, music, fashion, fads, and shopping.

Teenagers rule their own social space, too. As a group, they have come to expect a level of personal freedom that is limited only by their own sense of decorum and discipline—a remarkable shift from the days before the Second World War, when high school students were supposed to put their free time to good use, preparing for adult futures. In the 1990s, they assume they have what the papers call "a right to party" (whether they exercise the right or not), and they take it for granted that their teenage years are prime time to let off steam with their friends. When the National Highway Transportation Board considered setting a curfew for teenagers in 1993, for instance, in hopes of getting drunk drivers off the road, the suggestion did not get very far. "Getting arrested for not being home on time, that's bizarre," one high school student told the *Washington Post*. "That goes against your constitutional rights to . . . freedom." As another teenager put it, "This is America, the land of freedom. So don't restrict ours." They take the same approach when it comes to expressing their personal style, their values, their sexuality. "Nobody should have a say in who I am," a seventeen-year-old puts it plainly.

This determination to establish separate identities and to demonstrate their independence, one way or another, from their parents' world, often brands teenagers as potential troublemakers in the public mind—we tend to expect them to be hostile, indifferent, or messed up, victims of an increasingly complex world that makes them old before their time. We look at their grungy clothes, their nose rings, their tattoos, and we think the worst. We hear snatches of their music and wonder what's the matter with kids today? We pick up the morning paper and assume that the "burnouts" who usually make the news represent the high school crowd. A reporter for the *Dallas Morning News*, for instance, presents a typically bleak picture of the modern teenage world: "Children barely old enough to drive flirt with pregnancy and the possibility of AIDS. Students accosted at knife point give up their jewelry and $100 running shoes. Kids swagger through high school corridors, guns stashed in their belts." Although the reporter acknowledges that the image is overdrawn, the message is nevertheless repeated in countless newspaper and magazine articles, on television shows, in movies—a teenage crisis is at hand. What used to be called juvenile delinquency or deviant behavior now passes for everyday teenage life.

Wholesome Adolescents

This certainly is not the image that pioneer marketers envisioned back in the 1940s, when they first began to promote teenagers as a group apart. On the contrary, they usually portrayed teenagers as fun-loving, wholesome high school students eager to try out adult freedoms, but willing to live by adult rules. In fact, when they referred to teenagers, they actually had adolescents in mind, a term that dated back to the nineteenth century. According to the experts—psychologists and educators who popularized the idea—adolescents were awkward, vulnerable creatures, the innocent victims of raging hormones, rampant insecurity, and fervent idealism (which often bordered on arrogance), characteristics that were apparently linked to puberty and a lack of experience. Because they were susceptible to worldly temptations (like cigarettes, dance halls, gambling, and liquor), adolescents had to be protected from the adult world, ideally in high school. There they could work through the storm and stress of their teenage years in a disciplined, wholesome, adult-guided environment. In the process, they would discover their talents and goals, develop good work habits, and learn the value of respect for authority—or so the theory went.

The idea that high school guaranteed a healthy adolescence made sense from the experts' point of view. In the nineteenth century, industrialization and specialization had already put a premium on higher education for youth who expected to rise in the world: By the turn of the century, boys who intended to hold "good" professional or white-collar jobs needed a high school diploma just to get started. But at the time, the majority of families could not afford to invest in education. For instance, although the high school population doubled in the 1890s, only 6 percent of the nation's seventeen-year-olds earned diplomas in 1900. Ten years later, when about 15 percent of the age group went to high school, only a fraction stayed long enough to graduate.

But that was not enough, experts insisted. A high school system that ignored the bulk of teenage youth could not produce the literate workforce employers demanded. And a teenage majority left to fend for themselves would not develop the personality, skills, and internal fortitude they needed to survive in a competitive world. Part of the problem could be traced to the schools themselves. High schools offered a classical curriculum designed to serve college-bound students only: Latin, Greek, English literature, history, algebra, geometry, physics, and chemistry. If high schools wanted to attract a broad teenage public, then experts would have to design programs with teenage tastes in mind—a "progressive" philosophy that began to take hold around the 1920s. Emphasizing poise and personality, along with Latin and Greek, high schools began to offer practical courses that students wanted to take, including home economics, stenography, typing, and bookkeeping. The investment paid off in increasing enrollments—by 1930 almost half the teenage population were high school students. Within ten years, a majority of seventeen-year-olds had earned diplomas.

The teenage market that began its spectacular takeoff in the 1940s was the commercial expression of this progressive philosophy. Since high school fashions, fads, and social life apparently kept students interested and involved in school, why not offer students a full array of high school products to choose from? Adolescents would not only learn how to become careful shoppers (a goal that seemed particularly important for girls, who would be raising families soon enough), but they would also have no reason to rush into adult life or adopt what the experts called "precocious" styles—styles that allowed them to look (and often act) much older than they really were. Envisioning the teenage market as an after-school extension of a home economics class, pioneer promoters took it for granted that adults could shape teenage tastes and steer young consumers along appropriate, wholesome paths—a theory known at the time as character building. It was just a matter of finding the right mix of teenage choice and adult guidance to help the next generation find its way in life—and incidentally build up a healthy business in the process.

Mixed Messages

Consider the model of teenage life promoted by *Seventeen* magazine, the leading proponent of this economic venture. Styles were classic, teenagers were portrayed as wholesome and clean-cut, and advice was tailored to responsible high school students concerned with their futures, their reputations, and their parents' point of view. But since *Seventeen* was also trying to sell advertising space, promoters presented a different picture of teenagers to the business world. In this context, they were enthusiastic, indiscriminate spenders whose highest priority was to fit in with the crowd. High school students were "copycats," promoters promised advertising agencies, "and what a break for you." They "speak the same language, wear the same clothes, eat the same foods. . . . You'll see them shopping together, sipping Cokes at the corner candy store, going to the movies . . . together," traits that were apparently rooted in their adolescent stage of life.

Although these contrasting images made practical sense from a business point of view, they opened a Pandora's box of mixed messages that came to define the conventional version of adolescent culture. On the one hand, character builders like *Seventeen* expected teenagers to take life seriously. In fact, the magazine offered solid advice about preparing for college and future careers and treated young readers as full-fledged citizens with an interest in politics, the United Nations, and issues like democracy and social justice. On the other, *Seventeen* encouraged teenagers to define themselves through their appearance (and their dates) and ensure their status as successful teens by purchasing the products they saw advertised in its pages. At the time, the incongruity of these ideas went unnoticed—since advertisements for household furnishings, hope chests, and classic outfits (complete with hat and gloves, and shoes and bag to match) prevailed in the 1940s and 1950s, no one worried about the magazine's dual message. *Seventeen* targeted strictly white, middle-class teenage customers who intended to follow in their parents' domestic footsteps, and as long as this was the case, the teenage market could be sold as a means of training potential homemakers (and breadwinners) for the future.

Rebel Culture

By the mid-1950s, however, *Seventeen*'s respectable brand of adolescent culture had real competition—white, middle-class teenagers were not the only high school students with money to spend! Postwar prosperity had opened the door to an entirely different teenage world, one that was populated by working-class and black teenagers who had never participated in high school social life before. This demographic shift changed the nature—and the appeal—of the teenage market. Once a broad group of teenagers had the chance to cast their dollar votes (without benefit of adult guidance), wholesome high school life and domestic dreams lost their power in the marketplace. And once a mixed group of teenagers were encouraged to speak in their own, distinctive voices, they shifted the market's focus to an uncharted world of teenage passion and excitement in the form of rock 'n' roll, leather jackets, fast cars, and drive-in movies.

The change enraged adult critics, who mourned the passing of "vanishing adolescents" and decried the rise of "teenage tyrants." Even well-brought-up teenagers were rejecting their status as adults-in-training. Instead, they embraced a teenage rebel culture of risk, romance, and relaxation—cruising in their cars when they should have been doing homework, hanging out on the streets as if they had nothing better to do, drinking beer and going steady, even though this kind of behavior only led to trouble. Thanks to the rise of rock 'n' roll (the most successful teenage product to date), teenagers had lost their innocence and their direction, critics believed, and juvenile delinquency had taken over the nation!

Teens Take the Lead

As the number of teenagers began to soar in the late 1950s, however, these criticisms lost their sting, and by the 1960s the economic value of the teenage market silenced all but the most determined critics. Rebels or not, baby-boom teenagers demonstrated an unprecedented ability to open their parents' wallets, and that made all the difference in the adult world of commerce. Whether they were screaming for the Beatles, protesting an unpopular war, or experimenting with a counterculture of sex, drugs, and rock 'n' roll, teenagers were now the center of commercial attention. "Social change started moving *up* through the age groups," a demographer explained. "Adults started imitating teens." In the process, youth replaced age as the font of social wisdom, and exuberance replaced experience as a key political value, or so it seemed at the time.

From that point forward, teenagers began to shape their own space and chart their own futures without reference to their parents' plans. Rejecting the rigid family roles that had shaped adolescent culture since its nineteenth-century start, they also refused to follow hypocritical social rules that had forced earlier generations to camouflage their real identities (and behavior). After the 1960s, high school students tended to lose their virginity earlier (and in larger numbers) than their predecessors had, and they considered alcohol a rite of teenage passage, not an indication of pathological distress, as adults usually assumed. And after the 1960s, teenagers no longer feigned wholesome innocence for their parents' sake. They knew about divorce, birth control, abortion, homosexuality—subjects that were rarely acknowledged, let alone discussed, in earlier eras. Commenting on the change in 1992, one mother was struck by the candor of modern teenage life. "Condoms! A few years ago you would never hear me say that word. It used to be whispered. . . . Now it's gone prime time."

After the 1960s, teenagers also took their place as a respected and dependable "niche" market—one that would wax and wane along with population trends like any other. Brought up from a very young age to be consumers, not producers, post-1960s teenagers expected to live and dress well. Thirteen-year-olds with a wardrobe of $40 designer jeans were not unusual by the 1980s, and neither were junior high students with their own telephones, televisions, and complete stereo systems. And they did not have to grow up in affluent families either. "Sometimes my mom punishes me by making me go to my room," the adolescent daughter of two hardworking high school dropouts told a reporter in 1993. "But that's o.k.," she said, since the room was equipped with a television, a VCR, Nintendo, books, magazines, a telephone line, "and a bunch of other stuff." Quintessential consumers, today's teenagers take it for granted that they (and their parents) were born to shop.

Ironically, though, they are also the first postwar generation to have serious qualms about their economic future. In an age of automation, plant closings, corporate downsizing, and dual-career families, they are learning the hard way that middle-class comforts are not guaranteed. Indeed, ambitious teenagers who came of age in the 1980s and 1990s were already well aware that they would have to make money (and plenty of it) to live almost as well as their parents did—a sharp contrast to 1960s radicals, who felt no compulsion to find a job and disdained the very idea of joining the "rat race." Those with no taste or talent for schoolwork, or no interest in science and the technical world, face the greatest obstacles. For unlike their predecessors in the 1950s and 1960s, who could at least look forward to good manufacturing jobs, regardless of how they spent their teenage years, teens today cannot expect to support themselves (let alone a family) without a solid education.

This economic wake-up call has fashioned a new public image for teenagers. No longer amusing adolescents eager to ape adult styles or cultural rebels in conflict with society's constraints, in the 1990s teenagers are presumed to be a mixed bag of independent, risk-taking individuals, forced to grow up too fast in a dangerous, demanding world. Today young teenagers are expected to decide for themselves at a very young age how to live their lives and which road to travel to adulthood—a dramatic reversal of the sheltered, wholesome, adult-guided adolescent formula. "They still have the same issues of identity and self-loathing and all that psychological stuff that J.D. Salinger wrote about [in *The Catcher in the Rye*]," a television producer explained in 1994, "but you're dealing with a different playing field.". . .

The Big Picture

[Each era] witnessed a significant change in teenage life that altered the concept of growing up for the next generation: the notion of "democratic" family life in the 1930s, which promised teenage children a voice and vote in their own affairs; the emergence of high school social life as a "typical" teenage experience in the 1940s; the vast expansion of the commercial marketplace in the 1950s and early 1960s, which opened the doors of teenage culture to whole new segments of the age group; and the transformation of mainstream middle-class high school students in the late 1960s and early 1970s from adolescents more or less willing to play by society's rules to teenagers determined to escape the social conventions that had trapped their parents.

At the same time, a rapidly changing social structure reshaped teenage visions of the future and influenced their approach to everyday life. The explosion of manufacturing jobs in the 1940s and 1950s, for instance, gave boys with no interest or aptitude for school a solid chance to make a living, whether they finished high school or not—an economic aberration that gave a healthy boost to teenage "rebel" culture. The opening of professional opportunities to college-educated females (coupled with advances in reliable birth control) gave "nice" girls their first real chance to decide for themselves who and what they wanted to be, options that ultimately revolutionized the structure of family life. And the breaking down of racial barriers in the 1950s and 1960s (thanks to efforts of civil rights activists) not only opened crucial educational doors to ambitious black teenagers but also exposed the callous, hypo-critical, and unjust structure of "respectable" American life. In fact, it was this exposure—through television, magazines, and especially popular music—that set the stage for the turbulent upheavals that came to define youth culture in the 1960s.

We tend to assume that the rise of independent teenagers (as opposed to dependent adolescents) is really a tale of cultural decline and parental neglect. But in fact, the evolution of teen-age culture over the past fifty years is a story of institution building, market expansion, racial desegregation, and family restructuring. Bombarded as we are today with stories of armed teenagers in high school, pregnant teenagers with no plans for the future, and self-destructive teenagers who drink and drive despite the yearly ritual of high school funerals, it is easy to lament the passing of a simpler time when teenagers respected their parents, high schools turned out educated graduates, and sex never reared its ugly head. But that cherished image of a well-functioning past tells us more about adult fantasies than teenage reality: The order and discipline we usually associate with the good old days had more to do with a lack of opportu-nities and alternatives than it did with a shared culture of "tra-ditional" family values or teenage respect for adult authority.

Time and time again over the past sixty years, teenagers have proved that they cannot be separated from the "real" adult world or molded according to adult specifications: Ever since the architects of adolescent culture imagined a sheltered, adult-guided world of dependent teenage children, their high school descendants have yearned to breathe free. In the 1930s, they battled their parents over curfews, cigarettes, and swing music; half a century later, the issues were sex, drugs, and rock 'n' roll. But the basic conflict remains the same, regardless of the issue or the era: Who gets to decide how teenagers look, act, and ex-perience life? And who decides what that experience means? Although adults often interpret this conflict as a simple attack on parental authority tempered by hormones and a biological need to stand apart, that is only part of the story. The evolution of modern teenage culture has as much to do with a changing economy, a national culture of consumption and individualism, and the age-graded, adolescent world of high school as it does with inexperience or hostility to adult rule.

Baby Boomers as the First Television Generation

Aniko Bodroghkozy

Two events fundamentally shaped life in the United States after World War II: the birth of the baby boomer generation and the introduction of television into living rooms nationwide. The simultaneous arrival of these newcomers into American homes forged an unprecedented link between them. In this excerpt from her book, *Groove Tube: Sixties Television and the Youth Rebellion*, Aniko Bodroghkozy analyzes the effect television had on the first generation to grow up in front of the small screen. Early advertisements for television promised a new medium that would educate young citizens, prevent juvenile delinquency, and promote family harmony. Skeptical social commentators expressed anxieties about TV competing with parental authority and schoolwork. Some even declared the end of childhood innocence and the beginning of a dangerous generational schism.

As Bodroghkozy illustrates, the burgeoning youth culture of television teens may have learned their disdain for the adult world from shows like *Howdy Doody* and *I Love Lucy*. Leaders of the 1960s' counterculture theorized how television influenced their vision of a rebellious mass movement. Far from stabilizing social and family order, the tube became a force for change. Eventually, however, many baby boomer viewers would end up turning off the TV set in favor of more

Aniko Bodroghkozy, *Groove Tube: Sixties Television and the Youth Rebellion*. Durham, NC: Duke University Press, 2001. Copyright © 2001 by Duke University Press. Reprinted with permission.

antiestablishment expressions such as art house film and rock music. Although they came to see television content as irrelevant, commercial, and steeped in a corrupt establishment, they still recognized the profound influence of this "sibling" on their lives.

Aniko Bodroghkozy is a professor in media studies at the University of Virginia. Her current book project is called *Negotiating Civil Rights in Prime-Time: Television Audiences and the Civil Rights Era.*

IN 1949 AN ENORMOUS RCA STARRETT TELEVISION set arrived in the home of writer Donald Bowie. In his "confessions of a video kid" Bowie, who was four years old at the time, describes the momentous occasion and how the installation of the set drew children from around the neighborhood to his house. As the delivery men fiddled with the knobs, a picture came on. There was Buffalo Bob, a grown man in cowboy raiment talking to a boy puppet in similar garb. And there was the clown Clarabell squirting liquid from a seltzer bottle right into the face of "father figure" Buffalo Bob. Remembers Bowie: "My friends and I were hypnotized on the spot." From the vantage point of adulthood Bowie hypothesizes that this children's series, *Howdy Doody,* "was leading us, while we were still in our single-digit years, toward adolescent rebellion." Surely the lessons for the juvenile audience could only be a celebration of antisocial behavior and disrespect for adults.

Another baby boomer writer, Annie Gottlieb, also remembered bonding with television. Like Bowie, she, the members of her generation, and the new medium of television moved from "childhood" to "adolescence" together. She observed, "Television was growing up with us, slowly gaining skill at delivering the images that would make us one organism with a mass memory and mythology. When Ed hosted Elvis in 1956, TV entered its inhibited, yearning puberty along with us. I was ten, and, watching the famed manoeuvres of the Pelvis—primly censored just below the waist—I felt the first stirrings in my own."

These baby boomer memories suggest a potentially subversive relationship between the medium and the first generation to come of age watching it. Bowie and Gottlieb described a symbiotic association: a television childhood learning anti-establishment values, a puberty sharing an interest in verboten sexuality. Television, as Gottlieb implied, forged baby boomers into a special community—one that recognized itself as such by the way its members all shared a common television culture.

Aging boomers reminiscing about their childhood from the vantage point of the 1980s were not, however, the only commentators who reflected on the special relationship between television and its first young viewers. A number of popular-press writers in the late 1940s and early 1950s pointed out the connection between TV and the tots. *The Nation* in a 1950 piece observed, "No Pied Piper ever proved so irresistible. If a television set is on at night and there is a child at large in the house, the two will eventually come together." Television critic Robert Lewis Shayan also used the Pied Piper analogy in his *Saturday Review* piece about children and the new medium published that same year. He went on to characterize television as a genie, with its young viewers as Aladdins. Television would grant any wish, fulfill any dream—all at the touch of a dial. According to Shayan, one of those wishes was access to the adult world. "The child wants to be 'in' on the exciting world of adult life," he argued. Television provided "the most accessible back door" to that world. For these adult critics, then, the connection between fifties children and television was a cause for anxiety. There *was* something unprecedented in the relationship. But what did it mean, and where would it lead?

From the moment of television's introduction into the American home, it was discursively linked to the children. Television, a postwar technological phenomenon, and the baby boom, a postwar demographic phenomenon, both led to profound political, social, and cultural changes in the landscape of American life. Arriving in U.S. homes at about the same time in the late 1940s and 1950s, these electronic and anthropoid new members of the family circle seemed allied in fomenting social revolution.

In the 1960s the phrase "television generation," which had first been coined in the mid-1950s, would function as a site of semiotic struggle over the meanings of youth in revolt. Diverse voices—from within the rebellious youth movement itself; from academic ranks, both administrators and professorial theorists; from the television industry; and even from the nation's vice president—all attempted to make sense of young people's rejection of dominant institutions and values by examining the generation's link to television. All agreed that television was important, but few agreed on how or why. Reflecting the deep generational divide and the seemingly unbridgeable gap between the ways the disaffected young constructed the world and the ways their elders did, the discourses about the meaning of the "television generation" were equally irreconcilable. "Television" became a sign, another marker of a generational battle that ripped apart the smooth functioning of adult and establishment power in the postwar social order of the United States. . . .

Coming of Age with Television

In the postwar period Americans linked the promotion of stability with the promotion of consumerism. If General Motors was doing well, then (at least according to the head of GM), America was doing well. American industry's return from a war-based to a consumer product-based market necessitated an expanding population of buyers. As Vice President Richard Nixon's 1959 "kitchen debate" with Soviet Premier Nikita Khrushchev implied, American superiority over the Soviet Union lay in the U.S. population's ability and eagerness to purchase household appliances. So as "homeward bound" Americans moved into their ranch-style, prefab houses, their generation went on both a baby-making and a product-buying binge.

One of the products they bought was television. Ironically, however, this new purchase would not serve as a tool for stability. Television would prove to be a force for change and upheaval just as would the suburban boomer children who so thoroughly embraced and found themselves linked to the new medium. As birth rates skyrocketed, so did rates of first-time television purchases. In 1951 almost one quarter of American homes had televisions; by 1957 that figure had jumped to 78.6 percent. By the early 1960s the medium had achieved a near saturation rate of 92 percent. The single greatest factor in determining television purchase was the presence of young children in the household. According to statistics, between the years 1952 and 1954 childless families made up 19 percent of new television households; families with teenagers accounted for 23 percent; and families with young children made up the largest percentage. Parents with children under two made up 32 percent of television purchasers. This latter group comprised the parents of baby boomers. Another study showed that although entertainment was given as the primary reason for the purchase of a set, pressure from young children was also a key factor.

The introduction of television into postwar homes created cultural anxieties marked by both utopian hopes and dystopian fears. Many of those hopes and fears revolved around the perceived effects of the new medium on children. Cultural historian James Gilbert has argued that in the 1950s mass media such as television became linked with anxieties about social and generational change. New forms of commercialized youth-oriented popular culture seemed to be erecting barriers to mark off a new youth culture incomprehensible and potentially hostile to adult society. In both the pessimistic and the optimistic arguments about television and its effects, commentators and critics couldn't help but assume that some fundamental change to the nation's young would inevitably result.

Television Utopias

In the utopian vision of the new medium, television would bring the outside world into the home. Television sets were promoted for their ability to be "your new window on the world" and to bring faraway places into the home theater. Those touting the benefits of television for children echoed this theme. Douglas Edwards, a CBS news analyst writing in *Parents* magazine in 1951, proclaimed: "With television today, the children get a sense of participation, of belonging. Contemporary events are brought to them in their homes. Korea is more than a tiny colored nose jutting out of the broad Asiatic face into the blue sea shown on a map in a geography book. . . . The chances are thousands to one that when you were a kid you never saw a President of the United States being inaugurated, [or] the great political parties holding their national nominating conventions." It is unlikely that Edwards, with his purple prose, could have imagined the impact on those same children two decades later, when television broadcast images of another war in a southeast Asian country and when the medium televised another national political convention—that of the Democrats in Chicago in 1968.

The theme of television providing children with "a sense of participation, of belonging" was particularly important. In the conformist 1950s, when fitting in and being part of the group were not only signs of proper personal adjustment but were also signs of good citizenship, having television meant fitting in. Edwards undoubtedly thought television allowed children to participate in the larger world of social and political events and that they would feel a sense of belonging to a world made smaller and more comprehensible through the new medium.

However, in the 1950s this notion of "belonging" through the purchase of a television set implied necessary and successful conformity. Baby boom children conformed by becoming television children. The advertising industry helped to construct the concept of a television generation by manufacturing parental fears that children without television would carry a "bruise deep inside." One notorious ad campaign pictured woebegone children who didn't have their own TV sets. The bruise that such children bore meant being "set apart from their contemporaries." In the social climate of the 1950s nothing could be worse. Thus television became one means by which to link this segment of the population together. Baby boomers would not only have their huge numbers in common; they would also have their shared rearing with the television set to knit them together. Television, according to social scientific research of the period and according to the discourses of the advertising industry, was primarily something for the children. Children without television were pitiful outcasts among their peer group. Therefore, being a well-adjusted, "normal" child in the 1950s meant possessing and watching one's own television set. And so the television generation was born.

Even as television was touted for its ability to set off a new generation of youngsters as more worldly and sophisticated than their parents' generation, the medium was also promoted as facilitating family togetherness. Rather than setting children off as different and incomprehensible to the older generation, television would unite all its members into a unified nuclear unit characterized by harmony and shared activities. Lynn Spigel, in her examination of advertisements for early televisions in women's magazines, shows how the industry attempted to speak to postwar Americans' desires for a return to "family values." "The advertisements suggested that television would serve as a catalyst for the return to a world of domestic love and affection." This promise may have been all the more seductive considering the dislocations and tensions of the war years and the immediate postwar period. Television-inspired family togetherness could be particularly useful in knitting children and adolescents firmly into the family circle. Parents and children would bond over their shared enjoyment of programming, thus eradicating any generation gaps. Television would also prevent potential juvenile delinquency by keeping "problem children" off the streets. Audience research suggested that parents believed having a television in the home kept the young ones from trouble outside. Proclaimed a mother from Atlanta: "We are closer together. We find our entertainment at home. Donna and her boyfriend sit here instead of going out now." Presumably without the television Donna and her beau would be prowling dark alleys, fornicating in the backseat of a Chevy, or mugging old ladies.

Television Dystopias

Despite these utopian visions of children's protoglobal villages and family TV circles, pessimistic fears abounded. Rather than bringing the young and their parental generation together, television, a frequently circulated anxiety asserted, created an unbridgeable cultural chasm between the two. Well-known social critic David Reisman acknowledged the gap in a *New York Times* article in 1952 but sided with the TV-molded young. He was quoted arguing that "refusing to consider the possibility that there can be anything of value in the average television program amounts to an announcement on parents' parts that they live in a different psychological and cultural generation from their children. If they cannot in good conscience share television and discuss the programs with their children . . . they should at least allow their youngsters the right to live within reason in their own cultural generation, not their parents'."

This notion of a cultural divide marking off the television generation from its forebears is central to James Gilbert's book on mass media and the juvenile delinquency panic of the 1950s. The trend toward a separate, peer group–oriented, culturally autonomous "youth culture," already developing at least since the 1920s, had by the 1950s achieved an unprecedented degree of social coherence and economic power. The consumer product industry had discovered youth as an identifiable market group, and, as baby boom historian Landon Jones points out, these youngsters were the first generation to be so targeted and courted by advertisers: "Marketing, and especially television, *isolated* their needs and wants from those of their parents. From the cradle, the baby boomers had been surrounded by products created especially for them, from Silly Putty to Slinkys to skateboards." This isolation could appear menacing to adults. Consumer culture and mass media encouraged and even fostered styles, fads, language, and—by implication—values and attitudes that appeared to place young people outside the dominant social and moral order. Gilbert notes a study on delinquency published in 1960 suggesting that this more middle-class form of delinquency "derived in part from an emerging youth culture fostered by a communications revolution and a burgeoning youth market following World War II. Its characteristics were pleasure and hedonism, values that sharply undercut the beliefs of parents. In other words, delinquency was an issue of generational struggle." Rather than bringing the postwar family together into a harmonious circle in which adult norms and values would be unquestionably accepted, commercial culture—and television in particular—drove a wedge into that circle.

Television seemed to destabilize the family circle by threatening parental authority and traditional parent-child roles. A frequently repeated worry during the 1950s was that television exposed impressionable, innocent youngsters too soon to a world of adult concerns. One study of children's viewing preferences found that by age seven children were watching a large amount of programming aimed primarily at adults. Variety shows such as Milton Berle's *Texaco Star Theater* and situation comedies such as *I Love Lucy* were particular favorites. Berle even began to sign off his show with exhortations to the young ones to go promptly to bed after the show.

According to media accounts, many parents expressed concern about how children were interacting with this new "guest" in the living room. Dorothy Barclay, writing in the *New York Times Magazine*, discussed the fear that television would supplant parents as the ultimate source of knowledge for youngsters: "Children get a great deal of important and accurate information from television . . . but is it too easy? Is this kind of learning more or less apt to stick? Is it too easily accepted? 'I saw it on TV' is now a statement of authority competing strongly with 'My mother told me.'"

Parental authority, therefore, would be usurped by a fun, new gadget that required of children no discipline, no work, no discrimination. Television revealed a world of adult concerns and adult entertainment previously hidden from innocent eyes, but it also, potentially, threatened the whole structure of adult knowledge and wisdom as the final legitimizer of parental authority. . . .

Growing Up Too Fast?

Fears that television was exposing youngsters to an uncensored adult world and that traditional authority was being subverted by the children's relationship to the new medium led Joseph Klapper to suggest an added danger perpetuated by television. Television would result in "premature maturity." Klapper, a media effects researcher from the Lazarsfeld school of communications study, worried that not enough popular attention was being given to this danger, which had child psychiatrists deeply concerned. He and other analysts worried that television gave youngsters a distorted view of adulthood or that it helped in "creating and building in the child the concept that adults in general are frequently in trouble, frequently deceitful, mean, and, perhaps most important, very unsure of themselves and in fact incompetent to handle many of the situations which descend upon them." Such portrayals may have reduced the amount of time children viewed adults as omniscient and caused them to find the real world of their elders wanting and full of shortcomings.

The idea of premature maturity held within it an essentialized notion of childhood innocence that television threatened. Children would no longer be real children. In this vision "real" children were submissive to adult authority, and the boundaries between the realm of childhood and that of adult-hood were clearly marked and rigidly maintained. Television's intrusion blurred those boundaries. The other side to this argument was the fear that parents would no longer be true parents because traditional notions of adult authority were supposedly being undermined along with the very right of adults to be authoritarian. If the new medium threatened to rob baby boomers of their traditional childhood, what on earth would this do to them? Leo Bogart meditated on the danger of premature maturity: "One wonders: Will reality match up to the television fantasies this generation has been nursed on? These children are in a peculiar position; experience is exhausted in advance. There is little they have not seen or done or lived through, and yet this is second-hand experience. When the experience itself comes, it is watered down, for it has already been half-lived, but never truly felt."

By the mid-to-late 1960s, when the first wave of baby boomers hit college campuses, numerous answers were offered up to explain how this generation was or was not dealing with a reality that proved so different from its television fantasies. For this generation had not turned out as expected. In 1959 University of California president Clark Kerr had asserted: "The employers will love this generation. They aren't going to press any grievances. . . . There aren't going to be any riots." He was mistaken. Large numbers of middle-class, white baby boomers who came to adolescence and young adulthood in this period helped cause a social, cultural, and political crisis unlike anything seen in American history since the Civil War. Indeed, the United States from around 1966 to 1971 convulsed through a generational civil war. Over and over again the question arose: how had this happened? How had this generation—the most wanted, the best housed and fed, the best educated, the most economically privileged group of young white people ever raised in this most prosperous of nations—turned into such a raucous, riotous, disrespectful, distrustful, disaffected bunch of potential revolutionaries?

One answer was television. Depending on one's point of view, television was to be either praised or blamed for causing or assisting in the disaffected nature of many sixties youth. Understandably, adult commentators despaired and raged at television's effects on youth—that concern went back to the 1950s. More interesting was the fact that a significant number of disaffected young people—activists at antiwar rallies, writers for the underground press, video "guerrillas"—were also making sense of their generation's rebelliousness through its relationship to television. As the next section illustrates, activist youth, seeing their generation in revolt, looked back to their fifties childhoods spent watching *Howdy Doody*, sitcoms, game shows, and other programming. That experience served as a powerful explanatory mechanism to account for their profound alienation from and revolt against the dominant social order.

Television: Revolutionary Instigator?

This sense of shared consciousness via television was poignantly demonstrated in a speech delivered at the 1967 March on the Pentagon. Thousands of mostly young antiwar protesters had managed to swarm onto the grounds of the Pentagon and found themselves face-to-face with bayonet-wielding federal troops of their own age group. Yippie activist Stew Albert tried to appeal to the soldiers. He suggested a link between the troops and the protesters by appealing to their presumably common (masculine) history:

> We grew up in the same country, and we're about the same age. We're really brothers because we grew up listening to the same radio programs and TV programs, and we have the same ideals. It's just this fucked-up system that keeps us apart.

> I didn't get my ideas from Mao, Lenin or Ho Chi Minh. I got my ideals from the Lone Ranger. You know the Lone Ranger always fought on the side of good and against the forces of evil and injustice. He never shot to kill!

Albert presumed that, as the television generation, those on either side of the bayonets shared a cultural link. Their childhoods spent with broadcast media should have instilled in them similar values and ideals, including a Lone Ranger who was essentially a nonviolent crusader for social justice. Albert's vision of a generation united through radio and television ignored, of course, divisions of class and race and evacuated women from the process entirely. Television was the great unifier, used by

Albert as a rhetorical trope to reach across an adult-created, artificial "system" that inappropriately divided media brothers. Albert and many other New Left activists refused to see that the federal troops guarding the Pentagon, like the young men most likely to find themselves in Vietnam, came from a very different class position. They may have watched much of the same television programming; however, they most likely formed very different interpretations of what they saw.

Although it may seem odd that an antiwar activist would attempt to persuade armed soldiers that they and their antiwar cogenerationists were on the same side because of television, the rhetoric wasn't entirely absurd. We need to take into account one of the dominant ways people in this period made sense of television as a medium. Four years earlier television had provided four days of continuous, uninterrupted coverage of the assassination and funeral of President John F. Kennedy. The networks made much of their medium's ability to keep the nation together in a collective, shared experience of grief and loss. One of the dominant circulated meanings of the coverage emphasized the power of the medium to forge viewers together into a unit. Nine out of ten members of the baby boom watched the coverage. As the first television generation, they were far more affected by the death of a vigorous, youthful president and its presentation on the medium with which they had grown up. The assassination served as an experience that united the generation—and the uniting process happened through the experience of watching television. Thus when Stew Albert appealed to his "brothers" on the other side of the bayonets, his rhetoric took for granted the unifying powers of broadcast communication to instill similar experiences and values in members of the TV generation, no matter what social roles its various members occupied.

Television Exposes the Adult World

Whereas Albert invoked the television program *The Lone Ranger* to explain the values all members of his generation shared, other youthful commentators used their exposure to fifties programming to slightly different ends. Some used television to explain how many in their age group had rejected the values and lifestyles of their parents and how seemingly innocuous shows had, in fact, served subversive ends in fomenting the later full-scale rebellion.

Jeff Greenfield, graduate of the University of Wisconsin, wrote an article for the *New York Times Magazine* in 1971 as a member of the "first television generation" looking back to the programming of the 1950s. Confirming Klapper's fears about premature maturity, Greenfield claimed that television had a particularly subversive influence on the young "because of what it showed us of the way our Elders really thought and spoke and acted when not conscious of the pieties with which children are to be soothed and comforted." He argued that from *I Love Lucy* and *My Little Margie* his generation learned that domestic life was dominated by dishonesty, fear, and pretence; from shows like *The Price Is Right*, baby boomers learned about greed; from the quiz show scandals they learned about the commodity exchange of wisdom and the fraudulence of that wisdom.

Greenfield's article appeared to confirm what Klapper and his fellow analysts had warned: television had helped to solidify for the youth of America a disdain of the adult world. From Greenfield's perspective entertainment television of the 1950s provided an accurate representation of the hypocritical values of the older generation. Fifties sitcoms and game shows were anything but innocuous, escapist entertainment. They were instructive pieces of information that young people could use to make sense of their world—a world they did not want to perpetuate. . . .

Television escaped the ability of those in power to control it, just like the nation's rebellious young were incapable of being controlled. They had been raised in their suburban neighborhoods to respect those in authority, to be obedient workers who wouldn't question hierarchy, and to reproduce the conformist, sterile world created by their parents' generation. Similarly television was supposed to be the great force for cultural indoctrination. An ideological hypodermic needle, it was supposed to inject its viewers with dominant views sanctioned by the social and political order. As Greenfield observed: "Television should have been a part of the pattern of increasing control of tastes and opinion; a source not of the greatest freedom of which rulers speak when a new tool for the amplification of their voice is discovered, but a new source of blandness, and imposed acquiescence to the will of the Elders." But as Green-field further noted, the first generation weaned on television didn't turn into a bland, acquiescent lot. This development could only mean that television wasn't doing what it was supposed to be doing—any more than many children of the baby boom were doing what they were supposed to be doing. Television and the children of the tube were both subverting the social order they were supposed to uphold. . . .

Television Content Rejected

This brings us to an interesting paradox. As I have tried to show, young people aligned with the youth movement, as well as alarmed adults, used the perceived link between television and its first generation of young viewers to explain the current state of the TV generation. On the other hand, this generation had by [the late 1960s] abandoned the medium to a considerable extent as a major source of information and entertainment. (Yippies Abbie Hoffman and Jerry Rubin were notable exceptions.) Harlan Ellison, noted science fiction writer and regular TV critic for the Los Angeles underground paper the *L.A. Free Press*, explained the situation this way:

> Walking down the streets these days and nights are members of the Television Generation. Kids who were born with TV, were babysat by TV, were weaned on TV, dug TV and finally rejected TV. . . .

> But their parents, the older folks, the ones who brought the world down whatever road it is that's put us in this place at this time—they sit and watch situation comedies. Does this tell us something? . . . The mass is living in a fairyland where occasionally a gripe or discouraging word is heard. . . . The mass sits and sucks its thumb and watches Lucy and Doris and Granny Clampett and the world burns around them.

The kids had rejected the content of television, leaving it and its irrelevant programming to their elders. Like teenagers and young adults of previous and succeeding generations, they watched less television than any other age group. For members of the student protest movement or the hippie counterculture, art films and rock music were the preeminent arenas of cultural consumption. Any self-respecting head or campus politico would be looked at askance were she or he to exhibit a too-hardy interest in the products of the Vast Wasteland. Hip and activist young people rejected television as a commercial, network-dominated industry hopelessly corrupted by the values of the establishment. The censorship and heavy-handed cancellation of *The Smothers Brothers Comedy Hour*, the only network program to succeed in engaging these young people, provided tangible evidence of the medium's corruption. . . .

A Generation's Paradox

Herein lies the great paradox of the first television generation. Despite the clear recognition by many movement commentators that coming of age with the medium had worked some fundamental transformation on the ways that sixties youth constructed reality and relations to authority, . . . most campus New Leftists and countercultural heads and freaks tended to avoid engagement with television to any great extent. Many of the era's young people actively rejected television as a useful source of information, amusement, or edification. Some found ways to eradicate network content and subvert "appropriate" uses of the medium in favor of foregrounding its formal properties when they did turn on the set—and themselves. Many also embraced their childhood histories with the medium and the ways in which *Howdy Doody* and other programs had inadvertently promoted their rebelliousness. Even as they turned the tube's programming off in droves, they still recognized their inescapable link to the medium. Television, as they saw it, was at least partly responsible for turning them into freaks, for causing them to embrace the values of the East as they rejected the values of Western consumer capitalism, for pointing out that the adult social order was nothing to look up to or emulate. Even hostile critics such as [college administrator] S.I. Hayakawa and Vice President Agnew could not deny the power of television in molding the members of this generation. They would forever be the children of television. As such, many would also find it impossible to ignore how the medium constructed their movement, their social and political disaffection and subversions, their alternative lifestyles, their idealism, and their threat to the established order.

2

EXAMINING POP CULTURE

Youth Cultures

Swing Music Inspired the Emergence of Teen Culture

Grace Palladino

In this exerpt from *Teenagers: An American History,*
Grace Palladino examines the influence of swing music on the increasingly specialized youth culture of the
late 1930s and early 1940s. Regular radio broadcasts
of live swing bands, dance hall performances, and
commercial records gave teenagers across the country
widespread access to swing, inspiring a shared style of
"bobby-soxer" behavior, dress, and language. While
advertisers and merchandisers discovered how to
profit from the distinctive teen market, authority figures fretted about the seemingly mindless focus of the
good-time youngsters involved whose tastes and values grew further from those of their parents' generation. Yet the still-wholesome image of the teenager
that came out of commercial magazines and Hollywood movies quelled any deep concern. Market
builders filtered the more threatening associations
with swing culture (sex, drugs, drinking) through a
sanitized middle-class lens that produced a wacky-yet-
harmless portrait of teen life that adults could toler-
ate. However, actual day-to-day life for most teenagers challenged this construct based on the
privileged conditions of an elite few. The experience
of Mexican American "pachucos" and "pachuquitas" is

■

a case in point. When noticed by the popular media at all, pachuco culture was marked by its difference from the middle class image and was most often depicted as sinister and dangerous. Yet Palladino argues that the hard edge and open rebellion was likely closer to the situation of most young people who could not afford to attend college or expect to inherit the opportunities of the upper class.

MORE THAN JUST A PASSING FAD, SWING MUSIC reoriented teenage social life and high school style in the early 1940s. Thanks to radio programs that regularly featured the most popular bands in live performance, it was easy enough to join the crowd; even the most sheltered high school students could develop a taste for "hot" musicians like Duke Ellington, Count Basie, Artie Shaw, and Woody Herman. Hepcats and jitterbugs, who took their music seriously (as opposed to squares, who did not), could easily spend two to three hours a night swinging to radio music, especially when a band was really "in the groove." Or they might spend their free time hunting down new records, or finding a place to dance. The most dedicated swing fans read *Down Beat* to keep up with the latest trends. The most inspired started bands of their own to play at high school dances and parties. "At sixteen I was jamming with a few sympathetic pals from the high school marching band," a fan remembered. "By the time I graduated from high school, I had, like thousands of other youngsters . . . given myself the start of an education in jazz."

Dancing the Lindy Hop, the Suzie Q, or the Big Apple (and showing a little too much thigh and enthusiasm for adult comfort), high school students gained national fame as "bobby soxers," the popular nickname bestowed on swing-crazed fans who were developing a new teenage style. In their saddle shoes, skirts, and sweaters, they became the new symbol of high school life, one that was identified with music, fads, and fun. Bobby soxers were known to swoon for Frank Sinatra (who sang with Tommy Dorsey's band). They gave each other "skin" when they met in the street. And they riled their parents with a maddening language that only their friends understood. Worse yet, they spent time and money organizing fan clubs and lined the streets for hours on end whenever a band came to town, just to catch a glimpse of their favorite swing musicians. . . .

The New Teenage Market

The fact that the population of fourteen- to seventeen-year-olds was larger than usual (9,720,419 in 1940) also gave high school students new visibility. Advertisers and merchandisers were beginning to recognize an attractive new market in the making, one that was not necessarily bound by adult standards or tastes. Celebrating the notion of carefree, high school bobby soxers (whose only concern in life was to have a good time and dance), they began to promote a new social type they dubbed "teeners," "teensters," and in 1941, "teenagers." Like bobby soxers, teenagers were tied to the new high school world of dating, driving, music, and enjoyment, and like bobby soxers, they were a commercial cross between authentic high school students and adult projections of what they should be: fun-loving, wholesome, high school conformists whose main goal in life was to be part of the crowd. Although it would take a few years for the term "teenager" to catch on in the popular mind, the concept was spreading rapidly, particularly as a marketing tool.

In fact, the roots of the teenage market reached back to the 1920s, when the high school population first began to grow. By mid-decade *Scholastic* magazine, the national high school weekly, regularly featured a few ads for goods and services that no discerning student could do without: athletic shoes, class rings, even life insurance to protect a student's future should a father meet an untimely demise. Ten years later the variety of products, and the size and frequency of the ads, had grown along with the student body. Now there were pens, typewriters, and books galore for schoolwork and leisure reading; gym clothes, athletic equipment, and shoes for every sport. There was also a growing line of products that promised to improve a student's social life. Planters Peanuts, for instance, would deliver popularity; Fleischmann's yeast could clear up complexion problems that stood in the way of romance; even Postum, a grain beverage substitute for coffee, offered students a path to beauty and social acceptance through good health.

But it took the swing music craze (and the economic revival it heralded) to move the staid and respectable high school market into more volatile teenage turf. The shift in style and tone was startling. In 1930, the editors of *Scholastic* had boasted a "high opinion of high school students . . . whose tastes are civilized, whose aims are important, and whose ambitions are serious." In 1935, the magazine warned high school students against mindless, extravagant consumption, pointing out that "any nitwit can spend . . . money he hasn't earned for things that tickle his palate . . . without ever asking why." By the 1940s, however, voracious appetites for high school fashions and fads, as well as movies, soft drinks, and popular music, had put teenage consumption—mindless or not—in a brand new, favorable light. . . .

Constructing the "Typical" Teen

But if market builders were tapping into real teenage trends in the 1940s, they were creating them, too. For the teenage leisure world they portrayed as normal in magazines and advertisements still represented a very select slice of American life. The jive-talking, milkshake-chugging bobby soxers featured in *Life* magazine, for instance (who came to represent a national model of teenage life), were not run-of-the-mill high school students by any means. They were part of the wealthy sorority set, sub-debs who expected to marry well and join the ranks of high society. Part of the 9 percent of teenagers who could afford to go on to college, they could not understand why anyone might choose that dreary option—not when they could be having fun! That these privileged girls had nothing in common with most high school students, either financially or socially, did not matter to image makers, however. On the contrary, their carefree upper-class style set an attractive new standard for teenagers nationwide, who envied their freedom and their casual approach to the future, to say nothing of their clothes, their cars, and their free-spending ways. Age and desire were the building blocks of teenage culture, and teenage desire—for experience, for independence, and for fun—was widespread.

Not that there was anything wrong with that, as far as promoters could see. Even the experts at *Parents* magazine applauded bobby-soxer culture as the easiest way to keep teenagers interested in high school. At this early stage in the process, the teenage world was neither hostile nor rebellious: "Teenager" was just another name for an adolescent or high school student, a step up (but not away) from childhood. The term evoked a much wackier style than the earnest portrayal of adolescents in the past, but it was a style that adults often found entertaining. Popular radio programs like "The Aldrich Family," "That Brewster Boy," and "A Date with Judy," for instance, all analyzed life, love, and family harmony from a teenage point of view. In Hollywood, teenage stars like Mickey Rooney, Deanna Durbin, Judy Garland, and Shirley Temple were bringing the ups and downs of teenage life to big screen audiences all across the nation. In the process, their wholesome image and respectful style spread the reassuring word that teenagers and adults shared the same basic values, even if they danced to wildly different beats.

Family magazines passed the word, too, as they welcomed teenage readers to the fold. Sub-deb columns gave way to monthly high school features in the 1940s, and magazines like *Good Housekeeping* and *Woman's Home Companion* hired teenage reporters to keep young readers up to date. "High school's opening again," a typical feature began. "Grab yourself a chocolate malt. Tootle on your clarinet. . . . Snitch a jacket from your beau. Go in for giddy plaids, for suits, for peasant skirts and blouses.". . .

Hollywood offered an equally wholesome introduction to teenage life, one that starred Andy Hardy and his friends as proper teenage role models. A happy-go-lucky high school lad, popular with students and teachers alike, Andy was also a vital member of a very democratic family. In heart-to-heart talks with his father, for instance, young Andy had the benefit of adult advice, but he was always permitted to make his own decisions, and his own mistakes, in matters of life and love. Luckily, his biggest problems revolved around catching the eye of the new girl in town, although he always seemed to make his way back to the girl-next-door (who was more his type anyway). Andy was Hollywood's idea of what a teenager should be: adventuresome but innocent, high-spirited but respectful, and chiefly concerned with the high school world of dating, dancing, and drugstore antics after school. There was nothing artificial in this presentation of wholesome, teenage life. It was life as adults wanted it to be lived, and Andy was more than happy to oblige.

Beyond the Innocent Image

In real life, however, teenagers were rarely so tractable. They loved the music, the movies, the clothes, and the language that advertised their separation from adults, but they did not inhabit the wholesome, asexual, yet somehow totally fulfilling teenage world that adults regularly envisioned for them, and they were not always willing to accept the state of suspended animation their elders prescribed. Mickey Rooney, for instance, the star of seventeen Andy Hardy films between 1937 and 1946, may have taught moviegoers how to act like proper teenagers, but his own adolescence was a far cry from the earnest innocence he portrayed on the screen. As a teenager he was sexually active and spent much of his time in the company of adults, drinking and gambling.

Shirley Temple, another child star who grew into teenage roles, lived a more conventional life. Yet even she could not live up to her innocent, teenage image for long. "Shirley's first . . . silk stockings . . . were as exciting as any girl's," *Calling All Girls* reported when she was thirteen. "She's still not allowed to wear them all the time—only when she goes downtown or to a party." Just three years later, however, this well brought up, respectful teenager was sporting an engagement ring at the ripe old age of sweet sixteen. Barely graduated from high school, she was an experienced married woman by seventeen, a pattern that was not so unusual by the mid-1940s.

Hardly precocious deviants, Rooney and Temple were more typical in their desire for "adult" experience and independence than movie-manufactured "teenagers" ever were. After all, there was nothing innocent about the jive culture that first inspired bobby soxers and gave such a lift to teenage style. Hot jazz musicians with a taste for wild abandon and illicit drugs had improvised the language and the beat that electrified jitterbugs, but this influence could not be acknowledged directly; like commercial teenage culture in general, the swing music craze had to pass through the purifying filter of the middle-class world before it could be deemed safe for teenage consumption. . . .

Across the Tracks: Pachucos and Pachuquitas

For instance, Mexican-American "pachucos," the would-be bobby soxers of a less prosperous community, offered a very different image of teenage life, an image rarely seen at the time, outside of social worker reports or professional journals. Like other minority youth, pachucos were just not considered part of the "American" scene. The children of poor immigrants, they displayed none of the fresh-faced innocence *Life* magazine took for granted. Nor did they have any intention of fitting in with the high school crowd; in fact, they usually dropped out of high school at the first opportunity.

Surrounded by elders who longed for the past and ambitious community leaders who urged them to follow middle-class rules, pachucos were determined to go their own way. Like mainstream bobby soxers, they developed their own style of dress and deportment that set them apart from their parents' world, but their style had a defiant edge that challenged the notion of carefree, teenage innocence. For instance, their teenage "lingo" (a dialect called Calo) was derived from the language of the criminal underworld, and it never failed to draw an angry rise from parents and teachers who did not understand it.

Their distinctive clothes reflected the same notorious influence (and inevitably provoked the same angry, adult response). Pachucos dressed in elaborate zoot suits, with tapered drape pants, fingertip jackets, and broad-brimmed hats, a look that was popular with jazz musicians and gangsters alike. Triple-sole shoes completed the controversial ensemble, which pachucos topped off with an equally controversial hairstyle: the long, slicked-back duck tail, or notorious D.A., that adults would later associate with juvenile delinquents.

The girls (or pachuquitas) were equally provocative, in short tight skirts, sheer blouses, dark red lipstick, and black mascara; indeed, they embodied the tantalizing, seductive style that *Calling All Girls* found so offensive. "We didn't approve of it and we didn't dress that way," a woman from the same community remembered of her teenage years. She had to admit, though, that pachuco style proved far more popular than she and her "respectable" friends ever expected. Called "little tornados of sexual stimuli" by their critics, pachuquitas had no trouble at all attracting boys (and men) with their sassy attitude and aggressive style. In fact, they seemed to have discovered the basic key to popularity!

Life Outside the Norm

Nonetheless, these teenage girls resented the implication that they were morally suspect just because they looked older than they were. No matter how they chose to dress, pachuquitas were never "easy." They knew how to make a boyfriend keep his hands to himself—they had to. In this otherwise traditional community, girls who were known to go too far were banished from their family homes, no questions asked. "Mexican girls are full of fun, they laugh and joke with boys, but there is nothing bad between them just . . . because they sneak out for dates," a pachuquita explained, giving almost a textbook definition of teenage culture. "We ride around and sing and laugh and go . . . someplace where there's new records. So we get some beer and have a lot of fun dancing and talking and singing and stuff. Americans do that too," she said, annoyed that outsiders held pachucos to very different standards.

The clothes, the music, the beer, and the distance from their parents' world marked pachucos as teenagers, like any other, but their poverty, their heritage, and their skin color made their separation seem that much more sinister and dangerous. For some pachucos who were caught up with neighborhood gangs and turf wars, it was. "These kids are full of animal mad. They can't fight the cops or the gabachos, their enemies," a boy explained, "so to get the mad from their blood they fight each other." Knives and pistols were the quickest routes to neighborhood justice. Boys who believed their honor was at stake usually took matters into their own hands. Their girlfriends cheered them on, or stood by them in court if the police got involved. They were proud to be associated with "rugged gatos" (cats) who were not afraid to prove their manhood to the world.

Mexican-American teenagers were not all pachucos, and pachucos were not all delinquents, but the differences were lost on the mainstream world. Outside of their own communities, minority teenagers drew no attention unless they broke the law. For instance, although half this teenage group dropped out of high school every year, nobody seemed interested; this was not the kind of "bobby-soxer" story that *Life* magazine was likely to cover. Even their teachers were not alarmed or concerned; many took it for granted that "Mexicans" were inherently slow and not cut out for school anyway. Except for a few sociologists and youth workers, nobody cared that this teenage group felt no connection to the larger, adult world—not until trouble erupted, that is.

A History of Hip Hop

Greg Dimitriadis

In this history of hip-hop culture, Greg Dimitriadis
traces how the genre started in New York as a
performance-based art form. Young rappers, break-
dancers, and graffiti writers from areas like the South
Bronx and Harlem spread the word about parties in
parks, tenement basements, and clubs. These events
of the late 1970s and early 1980s emphasized impro-
visation and interaction. DJs, or rappers, would spin
loose and fluid performances using boasts and brags,
narratives, and call-and-response chants to engage
the crowd. It was not until the breakout success of
groups like Run-D.M.C. that rap became more
streamlined and self-contained. Music producers and
rap artists shaped songs to accommodate commercial
recordings rather than live performances. The popularity of rap skyrocketed, spreading to Los Angeles to
inspire a unique West Coast sound. Dimitriadis examines the emergence of other trends in hip hop,
such as the black nationalism of Public Enemy,
gangsta rap, and hardcore rap. This excerpt from his
book, *Performing Identity/Performing Culture: Hip Hop
as Text, Pedagogy, and Lived Practice* reveals hip hop's
evolving and complex history.

Dimitriadis grew up in New York hearing about
early hip-hop parties and shows during the 1970s and
1980s. After earning advanced degrees in English,
American Studies, and Speech Communication, he

■

currently teaches at the University of Buffalo, The State University of New York.

HIP HOP BEGAN AS A SITUATED CULTURAL PRACtice, one dependent on a whole series of artistic activities or competencies. Dance, music, and graffiti were all equally important in helping to sustain the event. Like many African musics and popular dance musics, early hip hop cannot be understood as aural text alone but must be approached and appreciated as a multitiered event, in particular contexts of consumption and production. Tricia Rose gets at some of this interplay in *Black Noise:*

> Stylistic continuities were sustained by internal cross-fertilization between rapping, breakdancing, and graffiti writing. Some graffiti writers, such as black American Phase 2, Haitian Jean-Michel Basquiat, Futura, and black American Fab Five Freddy produced rap records. Other writers drew murals that celebrated favorite rap songs (e.g., Futura's mural "The Breaks" was a whole car mural that paid homage to Kurtis Blow's rap of the same name). Breakdancers, DJs, and rappers wore graffiti-painted jackets and tee-shirts. DJ Kool Herc was a graffiti writer and dancer first before he began playing records. Hip hop events featured breakdancers, rappers, and DJs as triple-bill entertainment. Graffiti writers drew murals for DJ's stage platforms and designed posters and flyers to advertise hip hop events.

The artistic activities that helped constitute hip hop, thus, were multiple and varied, though entirely integrated by and through these "stylistic continuities." In a fairly recent issue of *Rap Pages*, Harry Allen notes that these were "mutually supporting art forms" and "each gave the other resonance and depth." This sense of stylistic continuity was implicitly acknowledged by writers such as Steven Hager, whose 1984 book *Hip Hop* was subtitled "The Illustrated History of Break Dancing, Rap Music, and Graffiti."

The role of the artist was relatively diverse at this point in time. There were many ways to participate in the culture, though they all demanded engaging in situated activities.

Events took place in parks, tenement basements, high school gyms, and especially clubs like Harlem World, Club 371, Disco Fever, and the Funhouse. Accessing the scene meant accessing such places, in ghettoized New York City areas like the South Bronx and Harlem—areas ravaged by failed attempts at urban renewal and general deindustrialization. Unlike the current rap scene, this participation went beyond the production and circulation of musical texts alone to include practices such as dance and other face-to-face community-building activities. Though I will take a more focused approach here, it is critical to note that this performative ethic was linked, more broadly, to the music-making practices of the African-Caribbean diaspora. In fact, early DJs Kool Herc and Grandmaster Flash traced direct, familial lines to Jamaica, where "sound system" parties resembled these early hip-hop jams quite closely.

Rap's indissoluble connection with live performance is evinced, quite clearly, on early rap singles (1979–1982) as well as on bootleg tapes from early shows, from groups like the Fantastic Five and artists such as Busy Bee. The performative spaces mentioned above resonated in and across these early texts. Singles such as "Rapper's Delight" (1979), for example, were full of the kinds of "floating" or "stock" phrases that circulated in and throughout NYC hip-hop parties during the mid-seventies. Examples include the now-famous "you don't stop," a then-ubiquitous party chant. Such phrases were public domain at this time, called upon and used by numerous artists in varied contexts. Producing an original text was less important than the rapper's or DJ's ability to "move a crowd." Producing coherent and autonomous texts was simply not valued. Bootleg tapes, when available, were a by-product of this activity, as were early singles. The performance itself was most important.

Like the live events themselves, the earliest rap singles were long and sprawling, with little sense of internal lyrical (or musical) progression. "Rapper's Delight" is, in fact, over 15 minutes long. These early recordings were entirely unlike the self-contained 3- to 5-minute narrative tracks that would become popular in the late eighties. Such singles seemed to run on and on and at some point to simply end—as if someone abruptly ended the party. The closure implied in the three-part narrative form (i.e., beginning, middle, and end) was missing. Each, rather, intertwined loose boasts and brags, with longer narratives, with (canned) artist-audience chants—tools ubiquitous in live hip-hop events. Such tools were loosely combined and delivered in live contexts as rap was a more fluid and open-ended expressive form at that point, a practice wholly linked to live events. These singles indexed such events as unfolding activities, situations in which a clearly delivered and thematic narrative might not be entirely appropriate to help "move" an ever-shifting and milling crowd.

The earliest hip-hop singles evidence this indissoluble focus on the occasion or event in a number of ways. First and foremost, the prevailing theme throughout these singles is partying, getting crowds involved in the unfolding event. Lines like "Come alive y'all and give me what you got" abound throughout, flowing in and out of the more structured narrative sequences, as in a live show. Concurrently, the pronoun "you"—i.e., the live hip-hop crowd—reveals a familiar and friendly relationship between artist and audience. This holds true for "Rapper's Delight" as well as for nearly all early singles, including "Spoonin' Rap" (1980) by Spoonie Gee, "Money (Dollar Bill Y'all)" (1981) by Jimmy Spicer, and "Supperrappin'" (1980) by Grandmaster Flash and the Furious Five. In all these examples, the "you" indexes the participants necessary to sustain the event, active agents who engage and sustain the culture in complex and multiple ways in particular sites.

In a helpful counterexample, the pronoun "you" would come to refer to a very different audience in years hence, as the form and function of the music changed. Most specifically, the "you" would often interpolate dominant society as a whole—for example, as in KRS-One's line "You built up a race on the concept of violence, now in '90 you want silence?" or Ice-T's "You don't like my lifestyle? Fuck you. I'm rolling with the New Jack Crew." Quite clearly, these were not the active agents who sustained the event by engaging in collective and situated activity. They were nameless representatives of dominant society to whom these products were increasingly available for consumption outside of clubs. Indeed, the early "Rapper's Delight" speaks to a music still aware of itself as a dance or party music, as a music realized in situated performance. It speaks to a music that indexes embodied participation in complex social activities, not wide dissemination in disembodied texts. Any other use of "you" would have been entirely anomalous.

This sense of the event, of the recursive nature of interaction and communication, is evidenced, as well, in the use of "call-and-response" routines. These routines were ubiquitous in live hip-hop shows and are also featured on nearly all the earliest rap singles. Examples include:

> Go Hotel, Motel, What ch'a gonna do today? *Say what?* (in-studio audience)
> Say I'm gonna get a fly girl, gonna get some spank, and drive off in a def O.J.
> —"Rapper's Delight" (1979) by the Sugarhill Gang

> When I say "rock," you say "roll," when I say "ice," then you say "cold"
> Then when I say "disco," you say "the beat," I say it's "like honey," then you say "it's sweet"
> —"Adventures of Super Rhymes" (1979) by Jimmy Spicer

> Before you hear the party people yell "Sugarhill"
> So what's the deal? *Sugarhill!*
> —"That's the Joint" (1979) by Funky Four + One More

These call-and-response routines give clear testimony to the intimacy of the club or party situation with which these performers were perhaps most familiar. Rap grew out of a dialogic and interactive tradition, one that linked artists and audiences in some concrete fashion. These important but largely ignored aspects of early hip hop become evident when we begin mutually investigating early texts and contexts of use.

Run-D.M.C. and Rap as Commodity Form

These call-and-response routines disappeared from hip hop during the early- to mid-eighties, a period marked by the rise of Run-D.M.C. and related artists. Run-D.M.C. was the first mega successful rap group, earning rap's first gold, platinum, and multiplatinum album awards (for *Run-D.M.C.* [1984], *King of Rock* [1985], and *Raising Hell* [1986] respectively). They were the first rappers to appear on MTV, the first to grace the cover of *Rolling Stone*, and the first to have a major endorsement deal with an athletic wear company (Adidas). Rap became a popular American music with the ascent of Run-D.M.C., one that circulated widely in self-contained commodity form. Rap came to rely more and more on the in-studio producer specifically and the music industry generally at this critical juncture. Producing self-contained texts became more important than sustaining the live and often multitiered event. The voice of the crowd, the voice of response and participation, was silenced as rap entered this much wider and more commercial sphere, most especially by way of privatized contexts of use.

Run-D.M.C. was the first in a line of rap artists for whom the recording—not the party—became the all-important focus. The history of Run-D.M.C. is, in fact, inseparable from the history of Def Jam Recordings and its various behind-the-scenes producers and businesspeople. Def Jam Recordings was founded in the early 1980s by Rick Rubin and Russell Simmons. Like other famous producers including Berry Gordy (from Motown) and Phil Specter, Rubin and Simmons helped craft and develop their artists and their images in unique ways. In many respects, the cast of characters necessary to sustain hip hop/rap as an event shifted at this point. As Howard Becker writes, "Every art . . . rests on an extensive division of labor" and this division is contingent over time. Thus, as I noted elsewhere, while break dancers and graffiti artists became less crucial for constituting the art during this period, producers such as Rick Rubin became more so, crafting the art from behind the scenes in important ways.

In a particularly telling interview, Rick Rubin commented that his biggest contribution to rap was "the structured-song element." He noted further, "Prior to that, a lot of rap songs were seven minutes long; the guy would keep rapping until he ran out of words." By separating songs into "verses and choruses," Rubin, along with Russell Simmons, helped to turn rap into much more traditional, commercial pop music, one with a focused lyric content and one that could be easily consumed in private settings. Rubin and Simmons brought an explicitly producer-based aesthetic to hip hop, streamlining this otherwise more open-ended music into a more commodity-driven one. Many of their efforts reached platinum-plus sales status, due, in large part, to this popular approach. The move to self-contained commodity form and away from the particulars of the event is evinced from the very beginning of Run-D.M.C.'s career, on their very first single, "It's Like That," released in 1983. . . .

Rap Travels Out

This move to rap music and away from hip hop enabled the art's locus of production to expand. Hip hop had been a localized music. Specific clubs such as Harlem World, T-Connection, Disco Fever, Rooftop, and Funworld (all in the South Bronx or Harlem) were at the center of early hip-hop activity. However, during the early to mid-eighties, the outlining areas of New York City such as Hollis, Queens (the home of Run-D.M.C.) became increasingly important, as did areas around the country like Los Angeles (the home of Uncle Jam's Army and the World Class Wreckin' Crew). The so-called suburbanization of hip hop began during this period, as a much wider group of performers and audiences began to have access to the art. Rap was now a separable discourse that did not demand a strict integration in live multimedia production. Artists were no longer performers first and recording artists second. In the face of this massive commercial success, the event was largely overshadowed by the promotion and propagation of select and iconic figures through commodity form, in ways that had implications for the idiom as a whole.

These recordings were often consumed by way of boom boxes. These large and bass heavy radios allowed young people to take music with them, to play it anywhere they chose. Yet, unlike privatized Walkman radios, these radios projected music to people who might not want to hear it. Thus, crucial questions about public space and the ownership of space through sound became increasingly important in the eighties—questions we can trace emerging in and through select texts. Indeed, L.L. Cool J (also on Def Jam Recordings) places the radio at the center of his musical universe on cuts like "I Can't Live Without my Radio," articulating his vision of race and masculinity through technology with lines like "Walking down the street to the hardcore beat while my J.V.C. vibrates the concrete." L.L. appropriates and celebrates this sense of rebellion when he raps of claiming space in his neighborhood by putting his "volume way past 10." A politics of public space and the ownership of public space became increasingly important and evident at this point in time. As Robin Kelley writes:

> The movement of young blacks, their music and expressive styles have literally become weapons in a battle over the right to occupy public space. Frequently employing high-decibel car stereos and boom boxes, they "pump up the volume" not only for their own listening pleasure but also as part of an indirect, ad hoc war of position to take back public space.

Again, with the rise of artists like L.L. Cool J and Run-D.M.C., hip hop moved away from a more place-bound activity to a more mobile one, allowing for a qualitatively new activity, with new political possibilities and constraints. . . .

The Rise of Racialized Masculinity

Rap's oft-noted move to masculinist ideals and values came as a parallel phenomenon to the proliferation of producer-based technologies. With the means of producing rap increasingly consolidated, questions of access (or lack thereof) became crucial. Tricia Rose writes:

> Young women [are] not especially welcome in male social spaces where technological knowledge is shared. Today's studios are extremely male-dominated spaces where techno-logical discourse merges with a culture of male bonding that inordinately problematizes female apprenticeship. Both of these factors had a serious impact on the contributions of women in contemporary rap music production.

By many accounts, including Rose's, women were an active part of early rap. Early rap artists included Sha-Rock (who recorded a few very early singles with the Funky Four + One), Pebbily Poo, Sequence (featuring Blondie, Cheryl "The Pearl" Cook, and Angie B), Lisa Lee, Debbie Dee, and Wanda Dee (all associated with Afrika Bambaataa's Zulu Nation). Early breakers include Baby Love and early graffiti artists include Lady Pink. Yet, none of these artists had much financial success and their careers petered out during the early eighties, right at the point Run-D.M.C. entered the picture. Rap began to be constructed as a more masculinist art form during this period, one that both largely denied opportunities for female access and opened a space for the proliferation of already existing and deeply misogynist cultural discourses. Indeed, while in years hence female rappers such as Lil' Kim and Foxy Brown would rise in prominence, their hypersexualized and often explicitly violent work resonated in a popular field defined *a priori* almost wholly by men. In fact, both these artists were linked (often paternalistically) to male mentors—Lil' Kim to Biggie Smalls and Foxy Brown to Nas.

L.L. Cool J, especially, began to wed aggression against dominant society (as noted in the above discussion of "I Can't Live Without my Radio") with an often racialized masculinity. He rapped on his 1987 cut "I'm Bad": "MCs retreat, 'cause they know I can beat 'em, and eat 'em in a battle and the ref won't cheat 'em. I'm the baddest, taking out all rookies, so forget Oreos, eat Cool J cookies. I'm bad!" By noting that his competitors are "oreos," L.L. equates a lack of aggressive vocal prowess and presence with "whiteness." The implication is that being (metaphorically, of course) aggressive, violent, and "bad" would make one "authentically" black. . . .

Public Enemy and Black Nationalism in Rap

The widening reach of rap music—the increasing importance of media and the multiple though privatized uses to which it could be put—also opened the art up to new possibilities around this time. Specifically, a kind of black nationalist identity politics became apparent in rap during the late eighties as its community stretched irretrievably beyond local boundaries. A brief example of how recorded media engendered black nation-building within the idiom will prove illuminating. Public Enemy released a song in 1987 entitled "Raise the Roof" off the album *Yo! Bum Rush the Show.* An aggressive boasting and bragging party track, it contains the line, "This jam is packed so I just figure, all we need is the house to get bigger." Chuck D later raps, "It's an actual fact, it takes a nation of millions to hold me back." There are very definite political overtones here and throughout the single as chaotic abandonment bordering on the riotous is evoked (reminiscent, perhaps, of Martha and the Vandellas's "Dancing in the Street"). Yet at best, the language on the track is coded, not explicit. The first-person "I" abounds throughout, reflecting the loose kinds of self-aggrandizement that were so much a part of early party rap. A radical social consciousness was emerging in rap, though it was tied to the local "party" tradition.

Public Enemy's next album, *It Takes a Nation of Millions to Hold Us Back* (1988), however, was quite different from *Yo! Bum Rush the Show*. Note that the more personal "me" from "Raise the Roof" has been replaced here by the more inclusive "us" reflecting the album's encompassing black nationalistic theme. Their political agenda became more pronounced on this second release as evinced by titles such as "Rebel Without a Pause" and "Prophets of Rage." Indeed, Chuck D and Flavor Flav wed a pro-black stance with Nation of Islam ideology on these tracks as well as on others, including "Bring the Noise." Terms such as "devil" and "black Asiatic man" abound throughout, referencing the intricate genesis beliefs preached by Nation founders W.D. Fard and Elijah Muhammad. The Nation of Islam became a pronounced force in rap at this time, its blend of militancy and pro-black ideology finding enthusiastic support among many young African Americans. . . .

Gangsta Rap—Redefining the Real

It is an ironic and uncomfortable reality that so-called "gangsta rap" emerged at almost exactly the same time on the West Coast that Public Enemy and other nationalist rappers did on the East. While many have attempted to draw sharp distinctions between the lyric content of "positive pro-black" artists such as Public Enemy and "negative gangsta rap" artists such as N.W.A., these groups share at least one characteristic. Both groups encountered and engaged hip hop as a mass-mediated, primarily verbal art form—one no longer continually negotiated and processed in live practice and performance. Public Enemy's shows, for example, seem less like small-scale community performances and more like major-label rock extravaganzas. Elaborate props and rigid codification all give their performances a kind of large-scale grandiosity foreign to most early—clearly less formal—hip-hop music. The group, for example, is often flanked on stage by the Security of the First World (or the S1Ws), a paramilitary "outfit" that carries fake Uzi submachine guns, dresses in camouflage, and does an elaborate stage show behind band leaders Chuck D and Flavor Flav. N.W.A., now disbanded, shared a similar aesthetic. The group made a similar use of elaborate stage props, including "Do Not Cross—Police Line" tape, which was spread across the group's performance space on occasion. The message, again, was "Do Not Cross" the line between those on stage and those off. Like many popular rock stars, both artists replicated their album tracks on stage ("in concert") with maximum amounts of spectacle and pageantry, formalizing the line between artist and audience as in much "classical" European music. . . .

A New American Outlaw

The gangsta rap narrative struck a chord in American popular culture, most especially with solvent young white teens. Artists such as Ice-T, N.W.A., Easy-E, Dr. Dre, Ice Cube, MC Ren, and Snoop Doggy Dogg reached platinum-plus status, prompting artists and record companies alike to attempt to replicate their formula for success. Part of the gangsta's wide cultural currency comes from the universally extractable nature of his narrative. The violent outlaw, living his life outside of dominant cultural constraints, solving his problems through brute power and domination, is a character type with roots deep in popular American lore. Indeed, the gangster holds a very special place in popular American imagination. He embodies such capitalist values as rugged individualism, rampant materialism, strength through physical force, and male domination, while he rejects the very legal structures defining that culture. He is both deeply inside and outside of mainstream American culture, his position not unlike that of African Americans in the Americas for over 400 years. It is thus not surprising that the black gun-toting gangster has had such limitless appeal for so many young males, both black and white. The "gangsta" is a romantic figure, a ready-made tool for teen rebellion.

In key example, Eazy-E's "Boyz in the Hood," released in 1988 on the album *Eazy-Duz-It*, embodies many of the themes and tropes that would come to define the gangsta rap genre, including the stress on money and crime ("The fellows out there, makin' that dollar"), masculine invulnerability ("Ran in the house and grabbed my clip, with the Mac-10 on the side of my hip"), and misogyny ("Reached back like a pimp and slapped the hoe"). In typical pop fashion, the chorus, "Cuz the boyz in the hood are always hard, you come talkin' that trash we'll pull your card" is repeated throughout. This kind of narration, which has a strong visual feel to it, allowed and enabled a number of popular artists working within the genre, including Ice Cube, Ice-T, and MC Eiht, to make a successful transition to film. These artists blur the line between "ghetto reporting" and cinematic fantasy in these films, as have many rap artists entering the realm of popular American culture. In fact, Ice Cube's first film, which in many ways set the stage for the "hood" films that began to rise in prominence in the late eighties, was titled *Boyz 'N the Hood*.

Hardcore Rap

The gangster narrative became an intrinsic part of the art at this time, engendering an entire musical genre. Its wild financial success has helped to shape the contours of rap's present landscape, the "language" through which rappers articulate their raps. Most artists today acknowledge the genre either implicitly or explicitly, as values such as "hardness" and "realness" now dominate across the board. "Hardcore" artists of the nineties such as Method Man, Nas, Redman, and Jay-Z all embraced the violently impenetrable outlaw stance on some level, though they have all proclaimed a love for rap as an art form as well. They all employed performance tools such as word play and freestyle-sounding delivery, though they are all operating on a popularly determined landscape, both in medium and message. . . .

Many "rap families" or crews pervaded the art beginning in the mid- to late-nineties with the rise of Wu-Tang Clan, No Limit Records (home of the "No Limit Soldiers"), Death Row Records, and Bad Boy Records. These were record labels or "organizations" that extolled a group or ganglike ethic, on record and off, with myriad effects. In fact, the prevalence of such "crews" prompted several high-profile feuds, as between the West Coast Death Row and the East Coast Bad Boy camps. Both camps handled many aspects of their artists' careers and each generated relatively stable group sounds and ethics—including ones defined in opposition to each other. Indeed, a series of shootings and murders ended the rivalry in the worst way possible—with the deaths of stars Tupac Shakur and Biggie Smalls.

Virtually Out: Lesbian, Bisexual, and Gay Youth Cyberculture

Joanne Addison and Michelle Comstock

Lesbian, bisexual, and gay teenagers are often chastised or silenced by heterosexist peers and adults. Hostile environments discourage some teens from sharing their identity with friends or family. Moreover, when teens do find helpful resources, they are often tailored to the lives of adults. In response to the resulting isolation, many gay, lesbian, and bisexual youth turn to the Internet to find connection, support, and opportunity for social action. In this essay, Joanne Addison and Michelle Comstock discuss their research on lesbian, bisexual, and gay youth cyberculture emerging out of cyberzines, discussion groups, and support services online. They explore how a unique sense of community is nurtured across boundaries of the "real" world and cyberspace, generating a place for queer youth to articulate their identities and assert their significance as important members of society.

Joanne Addison teaches rhetoric and composition at the University of Colorado at Denver and recently published a book entitled *Participatory Research in Basic Writing Classrooms: Cultural Studies, Feminist Postmodernism and Teacher Research at Work.* Michelle Comstock completed her dissertation, *Re-mapping the*

■

Joanne Addison and Michelle Comstock, "Virtually Out: The Emergence of a Lesbian, Bisexual, and Gay Youth Cyberculture," *Generations of Youth: Youth Cultures and History in Twentieth-Century America*, edited by Joe Austin and Michael Nevin Willard. New York: New York University Press, 1998. Copyright © 1998 by Joanne Addison and Michelle Comstock. Reproduced by permission.

Territory of "Youth": Youth-Generated Sites of Rhetorical, Cultural, and Political Practice at Purdue University. She teaches in the English Department of the University of South Alabama.

IN *COMMON CULTURE*, PAUL WILLIS CLAIMS: "Young people are all the time expressing or attempting to express something about their actual or potential cultural significance." This is especially true of oppressed youth groups whose significance, and more importantly whose existence, is continually questioned not only by the culture at large, but by the youths' parent and peer culture as well. Such is the case with most lesbian, gay, and bisexual youth. A population largely ignored not only in current research on youth but also in political debates concerning homosexuality on both the Right and the Left, les-bi-gay youth are often isolated and lack the means by which to articulate their subject position in society. As a result of this isolation and increasing access to the Internet and World Wide Web, it seems that more and more les-bi-gay youth have begun to employ technology in order to understand and express their experiences and demand that they be considered culturally significant members of society.

[There is increasing evidence] . . . of an emerging lesbian, gay, and bisexual youth subculture situated in the intersections between cyberspace and "real" space, or between on-line life and off-line life. This les-bi-gay youth cyberculture is composed of multiple real, virtual, and imagined identities and realities that are actualized on various levels at different times and places. These different times and places, or developing histories and spaces, are informed by and engage the material conditions and lived experiences of many of today's les-bi-gay youth.

However, . . . studying les-bi-gay youth on-line carries many risks, as well as benefits. Giving more attention to these already heavily censored sites risks further regulation and adult surveillance (most notably the Communications Decency Act of 1995 and its regulatory right wing anti-youth, anti-access effects). Yet, it is important to argue for the existence of this cyberculture because of its ongoing contributions by youth to larger anti-homophobic political and social efforts. As Donna

Gaines, a longtime advocate of youth, states, "Young people have experienced an erosion of their cultural prestige, their impact as a social force has diminished, they are losing ground in their rights and civil liberties." Les-bi-gay youth organizations are especially undersupported and overregulated, as legislators touting "family values" continue to limit youths' access to both real and virtual queer communities, as indicated in the state of Utah's recent legislation banning les-bi-gay student groups from meeting on public school property. Chris Thomas, in the May 1996 issue of the e-zine *Oasis*, writes, "For too long, adults, gay and otherwise, have ignored the problem of gay and lesbian youth—problems ranging from isolation to AIDS and suicide. Now, via the youth-dominated technology of the future, young gay people are finding one another on-line and staking their claim for attention and recognition." In response, les-bi-gay youth Internet sites such as Youth Action Online have emerged. As Christian Williams (age nineteen), one of the founders of Youth Action Online, explains, "For youth who have been abandoned by their families or, worse, thrown out for who they are, YAO can serve as both a resource of agencies and services to turn to for help, as an alternative to the streets, and as a place to receive the emotional healing and support— the understanding that comes from another young person."

In the following essay, we will discuss the challenges of doing research on-line in relation to the significance of the emergence of a les-bi-gay youth cyberculture. This will involve building effective geographical as well as historical frameworks through a discursive mapping of les-bi-gay youth Internet sites, as they are being constructed by their founders and participants.

A Unique Space for Lesbian, Bisexual, and Gay Youth

Any attempt to map cyberspace (meaning here the Internet and World Wide Web) has to take into account its fluid, ever-changing multiplicity. Sites and links shift and change according to where, when, and how one logs on, leading on-line participants to often experience alternating feelings of vertigo and euphoria. At the same time, cyberspace is often characterized in terms of fixed, concrete spaces: "netizens" talk about the various places they have visited, they enter specific chat rooms to engage in discussions of interest, and they meet each other at virtual restaurants, swimming pools, and sex clubs. These on-line experiences often cross over into off-line experiences. It is the intersections between on-line and off-line experiences that we must strive to account for when conducting research on the Internet and World Wide Web because it is these intersections that reveal the complexities and possibilities of a les-bi-gay youth cyberculture.

The Challenges of Internet Research

Doing so requires moving outside of academia's obsession with and reliance on "history" as our basis for critique and interpretation. Instead, we base our understanding of cyberspace and the formation of cybercultures on [Edward] Soja's notion of spatiality as "actually lived and socially created spatiality, concrete and abstract at the same time, the habitus of social practices. It is a space rarely seen for it has been obscured by a bifocal vision that traditionally views space as either a mental construct or a physical form." This is not to argue solely for spatial critiques of the Internet, but rather to argue for viewing it not only in terms of a history, but also in terms of a geography that frustrates any attempts at locating some Archimedean point from which to offer a centered historical map. The notion of spatiality is an important one to consider not only as a way of breaking out of current temporal frameworks in order to deepen our understandings of social life, but also so that in the process of doing research on the Internet and World Wide Web, we do not fall into simplifying it in terms of a concrete physical space that can be observed or historicized in the ways that we are familiar with.

Further, representing cyberspace, particularly the les-bi-gay youth cyberculture, as dialectical also challenges early efforts to map or partition off lesbian and gay subcultures. These often racist and homophobic mappings argued for the existence of "gay ghettos," where lesbian and gay men led "lifestyles" that were distinct and separate from more mainstream lifestyles. Our mapping not only resists ghettoizing les-bi-gay youth, but works to take into account the complexity of their lives—their participation in a variety of on- and off-line mainstream and countercultural activities. As cultural theorist Ann Balsamo discovered in her work on the Internet and cyberpunk culture, many youth who identify as cyberpunks also participate in other youth countercultural activities like raves and body piercing. Angela McRobbie, in *Postmodernism and Popular Culture*, also refuses to position the youth rave music movement in simple opposition to either mainstream culture or other music countercultures of the past and present. She claims, "[T]he old model which divided the pure subculture from the contaminated outside world, eager to transform anything it could get its hands on into a sellable item, has collapsed." It is time, according to McRobbie, for cultural theorists to begin noting the subculture's wider social connections to "otherwise conceptually separate spheres like the media and higher education." Electronic networks make it especially difficult and inadvisable to draw fixed borders between on-line and off-line cultures and subcultures. Thus, like Balsamo and McRobbie, we have taken care not to isolate or ghettoize the emerging les-bi-gay youth cyberculture, but have instead positioned it in a mutually constituting dialogue with often homophobic mainstream cultures as well as other anti-establishment subcultures.

Positioning this les-bi-gay cyberculture in dialogue with and in relationship to other cultures challenges claims that the Internet is purely a bourgeois space controlled by the military-industrial establishment. On one level our research takes issue with arguments such as that of cultural critic Donald Morton. Morton suggests that cyberspace is just another "bourgeois designer space in which privileged Western or Westernized subjects fantasize that instead of being chosen by history, they choose their own history." Instead of dismissing les-bi-gay youth websites as just more examples of corporate exploitation and surveillance, we view them as important sites for resistance, reproduction, and pleasure. And although many queer Internet and websites sometimes appear to serve as large cybercloset for an elite class of mostly white, gay, politically disengaged males, we have found that these sites can also provide powerful opportunities for resistance and political organization. It is this establishment of politically effective "social selves," a process both enabled and shaped by Internet technology, which marks les-bi-gay youth on the Internet as a subculture.

Constructing these Internet and websites as spaces for political and social resistance is not the same as denying their investments in elitist corporate structures and dominant cultural narratives. In delineating this cyberculture's prominent features, such as its reliance upon and use of computer technology, its "coming out" narratives and statements of identity, its anti-homophobic political positions, and its utopian fantasies of a world without shame and homophobia, we will discuss how these features are informed by social, cultural, and political conditions. Our approach also takes into account how subjectivities—raced, classed, gendered, sexualized—are articulated and experienced by youth participants, a question largely ignored by early subcultural theorists. Finally, instead of offering just one, totalizing vision—an adult researcher's perspective—we are engaging multiple views and alternate mappings of the cyberculture, based on how a variety of participants have experienced interfacing with it.

Engaging multiple perspectives, however, has been complicated by academic bureaucratic strictures on research in general. Research guidelines that are meant to prevent the exploitation of "under-age" survey respondents (a protective measure we both agree and disagree with) also serve to isolate youth and deny them the opportunity to speak for and contribute to the accounts of their communities that are being constructed by others. Further, in the case of les-bi-gay youth, it is generally not an option to obtain parental permission for them to be part of a research project, since most of them are not "out" to their parents or guardians.

In light of these concerns, the Internet offers an interesting research opportunity. Many of these under-age youth are establishing cyberzines, discussion groups, and support services through the Internet. In studying these public sites, we can gain insight into an emerging les-bi-gay youth cyberculture that we would not otherwise be able to engage. We have chosen our study sites based on high levels of activity (the number of "hits" or the number of people who visit and/or contribute to the site), as well as their founding, construction, and maintenance by youth instead of adults. Our analysis of these highly active sites will be intermixed with on-line and face-to-face interviews with les-bi-gay youth between the ages of eighteen and twenty-one who are actively involved in the Internet, as well as our own experiences as lesbian- and queer-identified women under thirty years of age.

By Youth, of Youth, for Youth

In what follows, we will be marking and positioning many of the sites that constitute what we are calling a les-bi-gay youth cyberculture. While there are a number of sites that deal with issues affecting les-bi-gay youth, very few of these were founded and are being maintained *by* les-bi-gay youth. We have limited our focus to the most widely used of these youth-moderated sites. The sites we will explore include four cyberzines (*Square Pegs*, *Elight!*, *Oasis*, and *Blair*), which are the most popular type of youth Internet site; an IRC (Inter-Relay Chat) Channel (#gayteen); and one on-line les-bi-gay youth services site (Youth Action Online).

As emphasized in the previous section, our study focuses on two broad aspects of this emerging cyberculture: (1) how its members articulate and situate themselves politically in relation to heterosexist mainstream adult cultures and other youth subcultures (including utopic visions of the future); and (2) how the sites represent and actualize a variety of gendered, raced, classed, and sexualized subjectivities and/or identities. We can begin to explore these aspects in terms of a les-bi-gay youth cyberculture by exploring the "home page" or welcome page of the sites listed above. The home page of any site is the first direct experience that a person has with that site and often contains a purpose or mission statement. From the home pages, potential participants can determine much about the types of discourses and action that are allowable or deemed appropriate by the sites' moderators (who, again, are themselves les-bi-gay youth). For example, YAO's home page reads:

> Youth Action Online is a service, run by volunteers, created to help self-identifying gay, lesbian, bisexual, and questioning youth. YAO exists to provide young people with a safe space on-line to be themselves. This organization was formed to provide for the needs of queer youth; the need for a rare opportunity to express themselves, to know that they are not alone, and to interact with others who have already accepted their sexuality.

These mission statements represent not only what the site wants to be or do, but also what the site doesn't want to be or do. It is important for YAO, for example, to state that it is "run by volunteers" and not by corporations seeking to build marketing databases. YAO also represents itself as a youth-only space, a "safe space on-line." From what threatening forces YAO is protecting its youth participants is only implied. Adults? Homophobia? On-line and off-line sexual harassment? According to its mission statement, YAO's utopic intention is not only to provide and achieve a "safe space" for youth (a space that must be reclaimed again and again in the face of on-line and off-line regulations and harassment), but to help participants reach a point where they can "accept" their own sexuality. It is this intention that marks YAO as a provider of personal emotional support for youth, an act that is just as much political as personal in its resistance to homophobia and ageism.

Relatedly, moderators of these sites, often in response to participants' requests, have become responsible for articulating not only what type of activities are allowed between les-bi-gay youth at specific sites, but who is allowed to participate. Staking out a "safe space" becomes tricky when posts are often anonymous and emerge from undisclosed locations (a typical chat group sender line reads "nobody@nowhere"). Recently, when a number of users of the IRC channel #gayteen started to receive mail of a sexual nature, the moderator posted a statement elaborating on the fact that #gayteen is not a sex-chat line and should not be used for those purposes as it threatens the safety of the users. One #gayteen participant we interviewed appreciated attempts at this type of moderation, saying, "I mean, it's [#gayteen] a pure issues thing. You don't have the problems that you have on gaynet where you get people posting for sex and stuff that's really inappropriate. It's just talking to people about dealing with parents, coming out, losing a boyfriend. I like to read that just to remind myself that there are a lot of people that are going through what I went through."

Queer Youth Cyberzines

In contrast to YAO, the home page for the cyberzine *Blair* reads: "Hey there supahfreak, welcome to blair #3. blair is a web-only superzine for kooks and retards such as yrself! come on in! viva la yoplait! we ate all the fruzen gladje." *Blair* markets itself as the magazine for "modern fags," "cyberfags," and "fashionauts." While YAO's purposes may seem more explicit than *Blair*'s, in fact the use of terms such as "supahfreak" and "kooks," as well as the name of the cyberzine itself (Blair was a teen-aged character in the TV series *The Facts of Life*), point to a specific group of teenagers who have appropriated and "queered" retro pop culture (such as the iconization of Pippy Longstocking in the third issue) in terms of fashion, politics, and technology. Although it may not be overtly political, *Blair*'s queer appropriation of pop, skater, and club culture works toward a refashioning of a queer youth self or image, albeit a gay, white, male image, in conjunction with and in resistance to these other youth cultures. When *Blair* provides links to "straight" alternative rock sites, like Verruca Salt and Lollapalooza, they are not only paying tribute to the sites and their attending countercultural values, they are, in effect, repositioning the sites in a new and irreverent context. For example, when links to the website for the Smashing Pumpkins (a popular alternative rock band) appear in *Blair*'s fashionzine *Sissy* (a spoof on *Sassy*, a fashion magazine marketed to young female teens), a reframing and queering of both the straight-identified site and band known as the Smashing Pumpkins occurs.

Most of *Blair*'s articles focus on those fashion codes which mark a person as gay or straight. An ongoing discussion entitled "gay or eurotrash?" opens with the following narrative: "i swear . . . some smiling guy comes walking thru soho in some tight Bundeswear ribbed t-shirt and like . . . red jeans, and a caesar hairdo . . . and your mind starts going *blip* *blip* and then all of a sudden your NEW BOYFRIEND starts talking German and hugging his girlfriend! what a mindfuck! it's so not fair." *Blair*'s resistance to mainstream adult heterosexist culture is also evidenced in its numerous narratives of "irreverence" to and "deviance" from dominant adult regulatory codes. *Blair* editor, richard, marks the zine's birthdate as the moment he was fired from his web job for downloading gay porn.

Deviance from adult culture, both gay and straight, is also articulated in *Oasis*, another popular les-bi-gay youth cyberzine, which features articles on the "Queercore" and "Outpunk" music movements. In a recent article, *Oasis* editor Jeff

Walsh described Brian Grillo, the self-identified queer punk lead singer of Extra Fancy, as "the anti-Christ to Judy Garland fags." Walsh goes on to write, "This bare-chested rock stud bangs away those stereotypes harder than he bangs his 50-gallon oil drum in concert; as if to say 'Sorry honey, it's the 90's, no more wallowing in victimization allowed. Get with the program'." The desire to mark themselves as different from adult and more mainstream les-bi-gay artists is articulated repeatedly in articles by members of the "queercore" music movement. In an earlier *Oasis* article, guest columnist Midol writes: "As larger bands and media take on more and more queer presence, the impetus of queercore gets lost in the perceived acceptance of homosexuality in popular culture. Even as gay people get more attention in general, the queercore movement is more concerned with making great music and spreading new ideas than, say, attending an Ivy League college or appearing in a fitness infomercial." Unlike *Blair*, however, *Oasis* provides, along with its articles on fashion and music, extensive coverage of news and events that have direct relevance to les-bi-gay youth, such as the recent stand by the Coalition of Concerned Women (a Religious Right organization run by Beverly LaHaye) against the celebration of Pride Month in schools. Walsh, the zine's current editor, also provides ample webspace for youth to respond to articles and to interact with one another as readers are encouraged to write and submit letters and opinion pieces, poetry, fiction, humor, and coming-out stories, as well as personal columns.

Another cyberzine committed to providing web space and a web presence for young les-bi-gay writers is *Elight!*, whose mission is to "provide a literary freelance publishing forum for gay teens." Providing space for participants to articulate their positions is central to many of these sites. This insistence on providing a space/forum where les-bi-gay teens have the opportunity to articulate their experiences *as* les-bi-gay teens points not only to the insignificant subject position our culture has assigned these members of our society, but also to the invisibility demanded by our culture of les-bi-gay youth as well as the dangers involved in articulating coherent social selves. Thus, many of the sites we explored talked about their aim of creating an environment where teens feel safe and of claiming space on the Internet where les-bi-gay teens can express their emotions, opinions, and issues as well as gather to take political action. The need to articulate social selves through the Internet, however conflicted they may be, points not only to a lack of opportunity for les-bi-gay youth to do so by other means, but also to their desire to differentiate themselves from the adult les-bi-gay culture as it has been popularly constructed. Further, creating this space for one another evidences the ability of les-bi-gay youth with Internet access to resist this positioning as insignificant subjects through the use of current technologies. This is not to suggest that this resistance exists only "on-line." As our opening quotations and numerous coming-out narratives on the net reveal, these virtual experiences lead to resistance in other environments as well. Indeed, even the most personal coming-out stories on the 'net are stories of political activism, reinforcing the notion that coming out as a lesbian, gay, or bisexual youth often means coming out as a youth activist.

Cyber Community

Many of the on-line youth participants describe the Internet as a virtual stage—a space and time to safely rehearse the coming-out process. For them, there is no clear distinction between their "net selves" and "real selves." One informs the activities of the other. For other participants, the Internet is one of the only places where they can be "out." An anonymous contributor to a recent edition of *Oasis* writes: "Because I'm closeted, it would be very difficult for me to be active for gay-rights. I really don't want to come out. Only about 5 of my closest friends know I'm gay. Anyway, I WANT TO HELP!! :) So . . . if there is anything you can suggest, or anything I can do for Oasis/OutProud, please tell me!" Many participants like this one are careful to note the divisions and difference between their on-line and off-line lives, claiming that being out on-line is not as real as being out at school or at home. For them, the consequences of being out on-line are not perceived to be as great as those of being out off-line. One participant we interviewed said he didn't want to join any on-line discussion groups at first for fear of becoming "one of those cyber-junkies" who spends all of his or her time at the computer. Because he was "busy coming out and meeting all kinds of people," he "didn't need to depend on the net for [his] social life." On the other hand, on-line participants, like Eric Wilcox, do depend on the Internet as a place to share or record their ongoing coming-out process. In a recent edition of *Oasis*, Wilcox narrates his crush on the guy down the hall, as well as his frustration with not being out. He uses his monthly column to speculate on and fantasize about the various ways he might ask someone out as well as become an active advocate of gay rights at his school.

What may induce so many youth to share their coming-out stories and their experiences as activists and as victims of abuse is the cyberculture's promise of "community." Just the names *"Oasis"* and *"Elight"* connote escape, nurturing, and shared knowledge. One participant we interviewed used the Internet primarily to escape her parents: "At the time [when she found the queer youth chat groups], I was living at my parents' house, and I didn't want to be there. I used to say, 'I have to go check my e-mail Mom, I'll be back in a couple hours.' And she'd be like, 'Okay.' And that was my escape." Walsh, editor of *Oasis*, describes his early experiences on-line in similar terms: "I remember it being such a rush to finally talk to other gay people on my home computer. I'll also never forget how alone I used to feel after I shut off my computer because that was the only place my gay community existed."

While "community" is a highly contested term, it is appropriate for us to take our definition of community from one offered in the cyberzine, *Square Pegs:* "Community exists where 'we' (people who have relations with people of the same sex—sex outlaws) converge." The use of the word "converge" (from "con" meaning "together" and "vergere" meaning "to bend") is interesting here as it suggests a coming together of different people at the same point in order to take action. This is, in fact, what happens as many les-bi-gay youth make their way through the Internet maze to find a point of community with others in order to take action on one level or another. For example, in the section of their cyberzine titled "revolution," the *Square Pegs* editors have provided links and/or addresses for the president, vice-president, and many of the Senate and House of Representatives members.

But an aspect that stands out in many of these sites is the express attempt at constructing an inclusive community, despite the reality of exclusiveness based on gender, race, class, and sexuality. The images and subjectivities represented on most of these sites, in both graphic and textual form, are exclusively those of white gay males. In fact, unless one indicates otherwise (i.e., "I am a 15-year-old black gay male" or "I am a 16-year-old white lesbian"), it is assumed participants are gay white males. This bias is especially evidenced in "personal ad" pages, where people can hook up with each other electronically as friends or "something more" (*"Elight!*—Personal Ads"). Out of the sixty-seven youth who sent in personal ads to *Elight!*, only seven identified themselves as women and only one identified himself as a black male. This situation mirrors the current social and material conditions of most females and minorities in relation to their access to and knowledge of technology.

It seems editors and participants do see gender exclusiveness as a problem on many of the sites. Walsh answered a recent *Oasis* opinion letter complaining about the zine's "boysey content" with the following statement: "*Oasis* has tried to increase the girl content on many occasions, and each attempt brings letters of interest, but none that follow through. We're trying." Also, the moderator of #gayteen concludes his welcome page with what seems like both a response to criticism and a plea for more female participants: "I just want to stress that #gayteen is NOT just for gay males. We have quite a few lesbian/bisexual females on the channel, and any more are welcome to be a part of the channel as well." The women we talked to about their on-line experiences spoke of gravitating from general "queer" and "queer youth" sites, which are dominated by males, to women-only sites, like Sappho, where they were likely to read about experiences more closely resembling their own. But even at these sites lesbian and female bisexual youth do not have space of their own, as these sites include women of all ages and thus seldom focus on issues specific to lesbian and female bisexual youth. Tellingly, our search thus far has not turned up any exclusive lesbian and/or female bisexual youth sites, although it has turned up exclusive gay male youth sites (e.g., BOY2BOY). As one young lesbian wrote in her Letter to the Editor: "I am a 16-year-old lesbian, and you are right, it is hard for us to find people to talk to and information to help us. Very little is done for gay youth and people on gay chat lines won't even talk to me because they say I am too young." Perhaps because it focuses exclusively on participant short stories and poems, *Elight!* appears to be the only site able to balance "boy" and "girl" content. None of the sites, however, seems willing to address the race and class inequities inherent in both the cyberculture and in the culture at large—exclusionary forces that determine not only who participates or who is represented in the cyberculture, but also who gets access to the technology and information necessary for participation.

Times of Terrorism: Teen Slang After September 11, 2001

Emily Wax

Six months after the terrorist attacks of September 11, 2001, Emily Wax documented a special strain of slang based on language emanating from the disaster. This "terror humor" is a contemporary example of the way youth cultures can absorb current events and quickly create their own responses to them. Whether such uninhibited joking ends up easing tension during a crisis or whether it serves to aggravate explosive emotions, teenagers tend to lead the way when it comes to innovative lingo. Emily Wax is a *Washington Post* staff writer who often reports on education.

THEIR BEDROOMS ARE "GROUND ZERO." TRANS-lation? A total mess.

A mean teacher? He's "such a terrorist."

A student is disciplined? "It was total jihad."

Petty concerns? "That's so Sept. 10."

And out-of-style clothes? "Is that a burqa?"

It's just six months since Sept. 11, but that's enough time for the vocabulary of one of the country's most frightening days to become slang for teenagers of all backgrounds, comic relief in school hallways and hangouts.

"It's like 'Osama Yo Mama' as an insult," offered Morgan

■

Hubbard, 17, a senior at Quince Orchard High School in Gaithersburg [Maryland], where students have picked up on the phrase from an Internet game.

"If you're weird, people might call you 'Taliban' or ask if you have anthrax," said Najwa Awad, a Palestinian American student at J.E.B. Stuart High School in Fairfax County [Virginia]. "Sept. 11 has been such a stressful thing that it's okay to joke a little bit. It's funny."

Language has always been as malleable and erratic as the day's headlines, and young people have always been some of the most innovative and playful in linking world events to their daily vernacular. But it's more than what it seems on the surface.

"When you have adolescent bravado and nothing can hurt you, underneath that is really a tremendous fear that everything can hurt you," said Alan Lipman, executive director of the Center at Georgetown for the Study of Violence. "What better way than humor to take these horrific ideas and make them go away?"

The center is doing an in-depth study of college-age and teenage students and how they got through the first such attack of their lives.

"My friends call me 'terrorist' or 'fundamentalist,' sometimes as a nickname," said Nabeel Babaa, 17, who came to this country from Kuwait when he was 3 years old and is now a senior at Sherwood High School in Olney [Maryland]. "It's not hurtful in the way we say it, 'cause we are kidding around with each other."

When Muslim students call themselves "Osama," Lipman said, they are trying to take back the power of being called such things, just like members of other minority groups who take negative words and use them on one another.

"They are trying to joke around, which takes the air out of it and shows how ridiculous it all is," Lipman said. "Then they feel a sense of connection over joking about it."

Only popular comics on television, radio and the Internet have as much influence on the national parlance as do brazen adolescents with their energy and uninhibited desire to craft their own language, linguistic and sociology experts said.

Teenagers breeze through such expressions as "He's as hard to find as bin Laden," or "emo" to describe people who are very emotional about Sept. 11. (It traditionally referred to brooding, pop punk music.) Girls might say a boy is "firefighter cute" instead of the more common "hottie."

And using Sept. 11 words to crack that well-turned one-liner or pithy witticism has calmed some frazzled nerves.

"We're able to make jokes and aren't as overly sensitive as before," said Jonathan Raviv, 17, a senior at Bethesda-Chevy Chase High School. "You don't want to offend anyone. But sometimes it's a little insensitive, and that's the nature of the joke."

Teachers worry that such slang could cross the line between funny and offensive.

"There was some concern about this sort of thing, and teachers are conscious of this," said Jon Virden, an English teacher at Bethesda-Chevy Chase. "It does bring up the issue of what is the lag time to laugh at something like this. But students were considerate of this."

The lag time after Sept. 11 was significant; round-the-clock news replaced all other programming, and laughter was rare. But the first "safe zone" for jokes and slang emerged—the enemy, bin Laden and the Taliban—and others soon followed.

"Terror humor," as it's called by those studying the phenomenon, is even going to be the subject of a special panel organized by Paul Lewis, an English professor at Boston College, for a conference of the International Society for Humor Studies this summer in Forli, Italy.

"Teenagers may be quicker to be more irreverent or raw and less likely to have their emotions repressed," he said. "There was a time right after the attacks when humor just stopped. But I thought the return of humor was very much predicted. Disasters don't take away humor."

Slang has always bubbled to the surface during crisis points. Some fades quickly, but some becomes a part of the national lexicon. And young people are comfortable being sassy sooner than adults are—think "going postal," "the mother of all battles" or "nuke 'em."

"Teenagers' language tends to be more vivid and lively than grown-ups' language," said Geoffrey Nunberg, a senior researcher at the Center for the Study of Language and Information at Stanford University and author of the book "The Way We Talk Now."

"Out here you hear [teenagers] say, 'That's so Sept. 10.'. . . Or, 'That's some weapons-grade salsa,'" Nunberg said.

Inside J.E.B. Stuart High, one of the most ethnically diverse schools in the country, students say they do use caution when joking.

"Since we actually do have students who wear burqas, it's not like we are going to say that," said Deidre Carney, 16, who is editor of the school newspaper. "But we do make a few anthrax jokes—like since there is so much construction going on, we might joke that there is anthrax."

Other students said it's easier to joke because everyone knows each other in a school that has no majority ethnic or racial group.

"If you do something to offend someone, then that's cold," said Ryan Hoskin, 17, a senior at Stuart. "But a lot of times we don't, and we are just looking for a way to deal with the crisis. It's like you need comedy."

Hoskin said that if a white student tells a joke involving people of Arab background, he expects to hear one back about the white students who were involved in the shootings at Columbine High School in Colorado.

After all, humor should help you through. But it should also be fair, he said.

EXAMINING POP CULTURE

Teen Consumers

The Media's Impact on Adolescent Body Dissatisfaction

Linda J. Hofschire and Bradley S. Greenberg

Teens are inundated with messages about the importance of their appearance. Studies have suggested that
media images of ideal body types produce negative
self-perceptions for women. Few of these studies examine the dilemma in relation to teenagers; this
article presents research specifically about adolescents. The evidence indicates that teenage boys and
girls might be particularly vulnerable to stereotyped
body images of the slender, toned girl and the slim,
muscular boy. Girls especially tend to become dissatisfied with their own bodies and engage in dieting
and exercise to change them. In some cases, this dissatisfaction can lead to unhealthy extremes such as
binge eating, anorexia, and bulimia.

Linda J. Hofschire's research examines the effects
of media on adolescent sexuality and body image.
Bradley S. Greenberg's foundational work about
sexual content in movies and television is widely
respected. In addition to body image research, he
currently studies relationships between parenting
practices and access to mass media.

■

THE MASS MEDIA PRESENT A NARROWLY DEFINED body type ideal. For females, this ideal is slender and toned; for males, it is slim and muscular. Although the current emphases the media place on weight control and muscle development help to promote a more health-conscious society, negative impacts, such as body dissatisfaction, preoccupation with attaining a certain body type ideal, and eating disorders, have emerged as well. In the United States, people are becoming increasingly dissatisfied with their bodies: A 1993 national survey of women between the ages of 18 and 70 showed that nearly 50% negatively evaluated their appearance and reported concern about being or becoming overweight. In a similar study conducted in 1985, just 30% reported such concerns.

Adolescents are particularly at risk for experiencing body dissatisfaction and engaging in eating-disordered behaviors because the onset of puberty leads to increased concerns about the physical changes of their bodies. Further, this period is also marked by increased interest in the opposite sex, and many teens strive to have the "right body" so that they will be found desirable and attractive. To the extent that the media define this right body that the opposite sex seeks, teens are faced with largely unattainable ideals. On television, popular actresses such as Jennifer Aniston (Rachel on *Friends*), Tori Spelling (Donna on *Beverly Hills, 90210*), and Jennifer Love Hewitt (Sarah on *Party of Five*) attract men with the seemingly impossible combination of a large bust and a waiflike body. And actors such as Scott Wolf (Bailey on *Party of Five*) and James Van Der Beek (Dawson on *Dawson's Creek*) regularly reveal their muscular physiques in the presence of women.

Adolescents' body dissatisfaction is a widespread problem in our society. In a survey of more than 3,000 high school students, 25% thought they were too fat and 68% were trying to lose weight. The pressure to improve one's figure is evident. A study of more than 2,000 high school students showed that 66% were doing something to change their weight. [J.J.] Brumberg [author of *The Body Project*] (1997) reported an even more disturbing statistic: "By age thirteen, 53% of American girls are unhappy with their bodies; by age seventeen, 78% are dissatisfied."

When considering the prevalence of this dissatisfaction, certain questions must be raised. Why are people increasingly unhappy with the shape of their bodies? What sources convince them they need to alter their figures? Researchers theorize that sociocultural factors are largely responsible for these high levels of body dissatisfaction and the increasing number of eating disorders reported, particularly among women. Current societal standards of attractiveness overly emphasize the desirability of a thin, muscular figure. Because the media are among the most prominent conveyors of these sociocultural ideals, it is important to determine whether they play a causal role.

Adolescents consume large quantities of media that emphasize these standards of attractiveness—for example, television, movies, and magazines—and it is possible that they apply these standards to their own bodies. Existing research about body dissatisfaction has focused largely on adult women. The purpose of this chapter is to expand on previous findings by investigating the relationship between the media and adolescents' dissatisfaction with their bodies. Further, adolescents are influenced by a range of sources other than the media. Therefore, two primary predictors of body dissatisfaction that have been identified in prior research—interpersonal sources and body type characteristics—are also examined. . . .

Media Effects

Research investigating the relationship between magazine readership and body dissatisfaction indicates that the media may play an influential role. For example, [L.B.] Newman and [D.K.] Dodd (1995) found a negative correlation for both male and female undergraduates between self-esteem and reading sports magazines and television and movie guides.

Other researchers have measured participants' body dissatisfaction after exposure to images of the thin body type ideal. [G.] Waller, [K.] Hamilton, and [J.] Shaw (1992) found that eating-disordered women overestimated their body dimensions significantly more than did normal women (i.e., women who did not display eating-disordered symptomatology) after viewing fashion magazine pictures of female models. In general, those women with more abnormal eating attitudes showed a greater tendency to respond negatively to the fashion images.

In a study of female undergraduates, [E.] Stice and [H.F.] Shaw (1994) found that exposure to magazine pictures of ultrathin models produced more depression, stress, guilt, shame, insecurity, and body dissatisfaction than exposure to pictures of average-weight models or pictures containing no models.

Very little research exists analyzing body types portrayed on television. A recent analysis found that the main female characters in 28 popular situation comedies tended to be below average weight and received significantly more positive reinforcement from male characters about their body shape and weight than did female characters above average weight.

Studies examining the effects of television have consistently shown a positive correlation between television viewing and body dissatisfaction. For example, [P.N.] Myers and [F.A.] Biocca (1992) found that watching just one half hour of body-image-oriented television programming (i.e., programming focused on the display of thin female bodies) significantly increased women's dissatisfaction with their figures.

In a survey of male and female undergraduates, [K.] Harrison and [J.] Cantor (1997) found that media use (i.e., television and magazine consumption), particularly magazine readership, predicted disordered-eating symptomatology, drive for thinness, and body dissatisfaction in women. For men, media use was associated positively with endorsement of personal thinness and dieting, and favorable attitudes toward thinness and dieting for women.

Another study also identified television's effects among both men and women. In a survey of undergraduates, [J.L.] McMullen found that regular viewing of popular television programming (defined as the top 20 shows in the Nielsen ratings) was positively correlated with depression after viewing physically attractive television characters.

[L.J.] Heinberg and [J.K.] Thompson (1992) examined more closely this impact of media characters on people's evaluations of their bodies. They found that women who rated celebrities as strong influences on their appearance were significantly more dissatisfied with their bodies and exhibited more eating-disordered behaviors.

Similarly, among college undergraduates, [K.] Harrison (1997) found that attraction to thin media celebrities (measured by how much the respondents liked, felt similar to, and wanted to be like each celebrity) was positively related to respondents' dissatisfaction with their bodies and desire to become thinner.

The few studies that exist involving adolescent respondents report similar findings. For example, [M.] Tiggemann and [A.S.] Pickering (1996) found that among a sample of adolescent females, body dissatisfaction was positively correlated with the amount of time they spent watching soaps and movies on television, and negatively correlated with their sports viewing.

The research on media effects reveals several factors that influence body dissatisfaction. Exposure to both magazines and television, as well as identification with media characters, have been demonstrated to negatively impact people's evaluations of their bodies.

In addition to the media, interpersonal and biological factors that have a significant impact on body dissatisfaction have been identified. In a survey measuring the importance of different entities on personal appearance, [L.J.] Heinberg and [J.K.] Thompson (1992) found that (a) friends were rated most influential; (b) classmates, other students at school, and celebrities came next; and (c) families and the general public were ranked least important. Researchers have focused on the influence of two of these groups: friends and family.

One study examined the influence of social groups on binge eating in two college sororities. In both sororities, [C.S.] Crandall found that the more a woman binged, the more popular she was among her sorority sisters. Peer pressure among the sorority members was so high that by the end of the academic year, a sorority member's binge eating could be predicted by the binge eating level of her friends.

The influence of family on eating-disordered behavior has also been examined. Through interviews with mother and daughter pairs, [K.M.] Pike and [J.] Rodin (1991) found that mothers of daughters with eating disorders were more likely than other mothers to have engaged in eating-disordered behaviors themselves. Moreover, these mothers thought their daughters should lose more weight than other mothers thought.

Body type, or body composition, has also been identified as a predictor of body dissatisfaction. This variable can he measured in numerous ways; one of the most common is the Body Mass Index (BMI). BMI is considered the most valid and reliable of weight indices, because it is highly correlated with independent measures of body fat. It is calculated by dividing weight (in kilograms) by height (meters squared). Generally, normal weight ranges fall between indices of 19 and 24; a score of 25 or more is considered overweight. A number of studies indicate that BMI is positively correlated with body dissatisfaction, that is, the higher the respondent's BMI, the higher her reported body dissatisfaction.

Research using male participants indicates that men are similarly affected by their body composition. Weight and percentage of body fat have been positively correlated with body dissatisfaction among male bodybuilders as well as normal populations. Because both interpersonal and biological factors have been demonstrated to significantly impact body dissatisfaction, they are used as control variables in the present study.

Our Study: Theory and Hypotheses

The principles of social cognitive theory ground this study. [A.] Bandura (1977) theorized that we "acquire attitudes, emotional responses, and new styles of conduct through filmed and televised [models]." If these models are reinforced, it is likely that we will mimic them. In the context of this study, adolescents may compare themselves to media figures who are rewarded for their appearance. If they feel they do not resemble these models, they may be dissatisfied and attempt to become more like them. . . .

[K.] Harrison and [J.] Cantor (1997) used social cognitive theory to explain their findings because modeling "provides a theoretical means by which [people] may acquire a body ideal, the motivation to engage in extreme dieting behavior, and the instructions on how to do so from the media." They highlighted two components of the social learning model that are relevant to this article—prevalence and incentives—to provide an explanation of how dieting behaviors and the stereotypical body type ideal may be socially learned from the mass media.

Prevalence is a relevant component because television and magazines heavily emphasize diet imagery and advertising, as well as slender characters. Because images of thinness and dieting dominate popular media, modeling of diet behaviors is a logical outcome of exposure. Incentives also are highlighted because numerous television characters are rewarded for their slim, muscular appearances (e.g., they receive attention from the opposite sex, they are popular, they appear happy and satisfied). Thus, observers may feel that they, too, will be rewarded by others and become personally satisfied by achieving the stereotypical body type ideal.

Based on social cognitive theory, it was predicted that (a) television viewing, (b) magazine readership, and (c) identification with female models and television stars for female respondents, and with male athletes and television stars for male respondents, are positively correlated with body dissatisfaction, belief in the stereotypical body type ideal, and attempts to improve one's figure through dieting and exercise behaviors. . . .

The purpose of this study was to measure the effect of media exposure on adolescents' body dissatisfaction. In popular television programs and magazines, physical attractiveness tends to be equated with having a slim, physically fit figure, and this "ideal" figure is frequently displayed. Thus, it was proposed that more frequent television viewers and magazine readers would be more likely to (a) express dissatisfaction with their bodies, (b) admire body types similar to the ones idealized by the media, and (c) attempt to improve their bodies through diet and exercise. These propositions were grounded in the principles of social cognitive theory, which suggests that people learn behaviors and attitudes by viewing models who are positively reinforced for their actions. A second goal of the study was to analyze media influence on adolescents' evaluations of their bodies when controlling for other significant predictors of body dissatisfaction. The hypotheses based on this theory were for the most part supported: More frequent television viewers and magazine readers expressed greater dissatisfaction with their bodies, idealized body types like those found in popular media, and modeled figure-enhancing behaviors (diet and exercise).

Interpretation of Results

With a mean BMI of 21, the respondents in this study were well within the normal weight range. [Research indicates] that normal BMIs range between 19 and 24. Despite this, the girls expressed dissatisfaction with specific areas of their body as well as a desire to be thinner.

The respondents also spent a significant amount of time watching television—the equivalent of nearly one full day per week. This result, combined with their low to moderate level of magazine reading, demonstrates that they are exposed to a steady diet of media that emphasize slender, fit people.

The results indicate that the types of television shows viewed, and not just the sheer amount, mattered most when predicting body dissatisfaction. Interestingly, total weekly hours viewing television did not have a significant effect on body dissatisfaction. However, more frequent viewers of body image shows or soaps were more dissatisfied with their bodies, whereas sports viewers expressed less dissatisfaction. Music video viewing also increased girls' body dissatisfaction.

The one area where sheer television exposure formed a significant relationship was in girls' choice of the ideal body type and measurements. The more hours of television girls viewed weekly, the more they preferred thinner bodies and smaller body measurements. Boys, however, were influenced in their choice of the ideal body type by music videos—the more they watched, the thinner the bodies they chose—perhaps because videos do not focus solely on athletic male figures.

Watching certain types of television also influenced respondents' attempts to improve their figures. Viewing body image shows, soaps, and/or music videos increased dieting behaviors, whereas viewing sports decreased them. Not surprisingly, respondents who watched sports exercised more frequently. However, soaps viewers were less likely to exercise.

Magazine readership also led to body dissatisfaction for girls, whereas for boys, frequent magazine readers chose larger body types as ideal. This relationship may be explained by the fact that boys were asked only about sports magazines, which emphasize muscular, athletic figures. Female magazine readers also were more likely to diet, whereas male magazine readers were more likely to exercise. The results for the girls support the findings of magazine content analyses, which have consistently found a strong emphasis on dieting.

Desiring to look like media celebrities also had a significant influence on body dissatisfaction. For girls, identification with models led to body dissatisfaction; the idealization of smaller body types, measurements, and clothing sizes; and an increase in diet and exercise behaviors. Identification with television stars also led to body dissatisfaction, idealization of smaller clothing sizes, and more frequent exercising. Boys were less influenced by media celebrities, yet those who identified with them expressed more body dissatisfaction and spent more time exercising.

Because other factors influence teens besides the media, it is important to consider the impact of these factors on body dissatisfaction. The multiple regression analyses enabled us to examine these relationships further. For boys, none of the media variables emerged as significant predictors of body dissatisfaction. Identification with media characters had no effect when controlling for BMI. In contrast, identification with media characters increased girls' body dissatisfaction even when controlling for the effects of BMI and magazine reading. However, BMI emerged as the stronger predictor in the regression equation.

Not surprisingly, boys who read sports magazines and watched sports on television exercised frequently. These predictors, along with friends' opinions about their appearance, were significant in the regression equation. However, only identification with media characters emerged as a significant influence on girls' exercising habits: The greater their desire to look like these characters, the more they exercised. Media variables were significant in boys' and girls' choices of ideal body types. Reading magazines led boys to choose larger body types as ideal, whereas watching music videos caused them to choose smaller bodies as ideal, even when controlling for BMI. When controlling for classmates' opinions, the total hours of television viewed weekly had no effect on girls' choice of ideal body type. However, media influences were significant factors in girls' choice of ideal body measurements and clothing size. Total weekly hours of television viewing led girls to idealize smaller body measurements, even when controlling for the body image shows, soaps, identification with models, and the opinions of classmates.

Clearly, marked gender differences were present in our results. Watching certain types of television, reading magazines, and identifying with slender or "buff" media characters tended to correlate positively with body dissatisfaction, with acceptance of stereotypical body type ideals, and with engagement in diet or exercise behaviors; these relationships were stronger for girls. Those boys who expressed dissatisfaction with their bodies had different concerns and methods for improving themselves. Whereas girls favored thinness and diet as a means for achieving improvement, boys idealized larger, more muscular figures and were more likely to exercise. It is possible that these findings reflect societal standards that socialize girls to believe that their worth is defined by their physical appearance.

Generación Latino: The Influence of America's Fastest Growing Youth Segment

Helene Stapinski

The styles and customs of Latino youth have increasingly gone mainstream, or influenced teen pop culture in general. The spending power of Hispanic teens has inspired companies and entertainment industries to market their products to this specialized market niche. Soon to become the largest ethnic youth population in the United States, young Latinos in some regions feel less like a minority group and more like trendsetters. Whether it is Anglo kids adopting hip-hop fashion, Latino beats thumping at parties, or Spanglish entering teen slang, Hispanic culture often takes the lead. Yet there is no single Hispanic heritage; appealing to a diverse population has challenged some companies to reinvent marketing strategies to fit a group with differing backgrounds. Helene Stapinski, a journalist and freelance writer from Brooklyn, interviewed teens and marketing specialists to document the new authority of young Latinos in the United States.

■

HISPANIC TEENS ARE THE FASTEST GROWING youth segment in the U.S., and they're redefining mainstream American culture.

Every weekend, 21-year-old Jovan Flores drives his black Volkswagen Jetta—with oversize, shining chrome tailpipe—from his house in Norwalk, Connecticut, to the tony town of Ridgefield. On this particular Saturday, with hip hop bleeding from his tinted windows, Flores is driving to the town's new skate park to meet some of his clients—30 little white boys who are learning to be just like him.

Flores, known as Face in hip hop circles, is one of the premiere break dancers in the New York area. In its second coming, the nationwide break dancing charge is being led by Latino youth. Flores, whose family hails from Puerto Rico, teaches break dancing to Ridgefield teens with the help of his friends Juni from Chile, Hydro from Colombia, and Double, an Anglo from Connecticut.

"When you're Latin, you're taught to dance differently because of the different rhythms," says Guillermo Perez, a 19-year-old trend watcher from San Francisco who's seen Latin-style break dancing spread to the West Coast. "There's different hip movement, different leg movement. You're moving so much that it's easy to just throw yourself on the floor and continue."

As Flores cruises into the Ridgefield skate park, it's easy to spot the nervous looks on the faces of many of the adults observing the scene. Clearly, the kids feel differently about his arrival.

"Face!" they yell, gathering around and practically breathing him in, molecule by molecule. Like Face, they wear their baseball caps turned backward, plus beaded necklaces, Esco and Puma shirts, and big Nikes.

In Ridgefield and across the country, it's not just dancing the white kids are picking up on. Young Latinos like Flores and his crew are redefining the way teens talk, walk, and dress.

"The music I used to listen to was lame," says 14-year-old Matt. "I listened to what was on MTV. I was into rock—Metallica, Rage Against the Machine." Now he and his friends prefer Nas, the rapper who endorses the hugely popular Latin-flavored Esco clothing line. "My mom was like, 'Don't get too much into that rap stuff.' But we break it out."

One 19-year-old of Norwegian extraction searches a mix tape for "that Mexican thing"—a song peppered with horn blasts. Another boy, wearing a colorful, South American-style woven hat, practices his head spin.

Flores shakes his head and smiles at the Spanish slang like "moms" and "pops" that colors his students' vocabulary. "If you talk to them now, you'd think they were one of us," he says, shrugging. "And the transformation only took six months."

According to Juan Faura of Cheskin Research, it was just a matter of time before Latino youth began to change the mainstream cultural landscape. "I've been screaming my head off for quite a while that Hispanic teens are the future of marketing," says Faura, director of transcultural research for the California-based market research company. [In 1999] 4.3 million strong, Hispanic youth ages 12 to 19 [accounted] for more than 14 percent of the total Hispanic population in the United States, and 13.6 percent of all teens. By the year 2020, the number of Hispanic teens will grow by 62 percent, according to Census Bureau projections, to 7 million, compared with a 10 percent growth in the number of teens overall.

When it comes to spending money, Hispanic teens don't hold back. [In 1999 they blew] an average of $320 a month, 4 percent more than the average teen [did], according to Teenage Research Unlimited. Overall teen spending was a whopping $141 billion in 1998, and Hispanics contributed $19 billion, or 13.4 percent of the total.

Already, because of their growing numbers, Latino teens are no longer a minority group in some areas of the country. "They don't view themselves as minorities, so their influences kind of rule the school," says Faura. "They're saying, 'You know, there are a lot of us here.' So they're mainstreaming their customs."

In fact, by 2005, Hispanic youth will be the largest ethnic youth population in the country. And the trend will only keep growing. [In] 2001, 18 percent of all babies born in the United States [were expected to be] of Hispanic origin.

Even slow-to-change, whitewashed places like Hollywood are beginning to acknowledge the existence of the Latino community—at least when it comes to how much they spend on entertainment. According to a recent report by the Tom S.

Rivera Policy Institute in Claremont, California, Latinos spend 6.5 percent of their entertainment budget on movies, theater, opera, and ballet, compared with 4.7 for Caucasians. That economic power is finally beginning to translate into starring roles for young Latino actors, although the gains are still relatively small. A May 1999 report by the Screen Actors Guild on Latino employment in Hollywood found that the number of film and television acting jobs going to Hispanics has actually declined since 1997. But it's no longer acceptable for someone like Madonna to play a famous Latina on screen, like she did in *Evita* [several] years ago.

Though she wanted the role of Frida Kahlo in the film on the fabled painter's life, Madonna lost the part to Salma Hayek, who [also starred] in one of the summer's biggest releases, *Wild, Wild West*. And Broadway star John Leguizamo, whose one-man show *Freak!* drew thousands of Latino and Anglo fans, [starred] in Spike Lee's summer blockbuster, *Summer of Sam*. Hayek and Leguizamo are further proof to Latino kids that they are part of the big picture and part of the mainstream.

That's a far cry from just a few decades ago, when Puerto Rican Americans like Cristina Benitez were barely accepted in peer groups. "People wouldn't know where I was coming from," says Benitez, now president of Lazos Latinos, a Hispanic marketing company. "They expected Puerto Ricans to have greasy hair and be slashing people's tires."

Anglo kids these days are much more accepting of multicultural ethnic groups. In a recent survey, 53 percent of teens said they have at least one close friend who is of a different race or ethnic group. Benitez credits increased communication and easier travel with helping Latinos hold on to their cultural heritage. "We're free to bring information over and enjoy it more than when I was a kid," Benitez says.

That information and the customs that translate along with it are not only acceptable to Anglo teens, but are now appealing to those in search of some cultural identity. An identity that may not necessarily be their own. [An] installment of MTV's cinema verite soap opera *Road Rules*, for instance, features six Gen-Y kids driving around Central America in a Fleetwood RV—dubbed "The Woodie"—decorated with Mexican tiles, a picture of Our Lady of Guadalupe, and rosary beads. They even have a Chihuahua along for the ride.

Trend analysts like Marian Salzman, head of the Brand Futures group at Young & Rubicam, have been predicting for the past year that American teens in general are putting a premium on refurbished culture. They're also in search of spirituality, stronger family ties, and a splash of color in their lives—three things that Latino youth culture already embrace.

"One of the reasons Latino culture is crossing over is because it's based on family values," says Benitez. "This is what the country is hungry for. What it's dying for. The stabilization of the home. But at the same time, the culture is fun and infused with emotion. You can have fun with your family— God, what a concept!"

Like most large cultural waves, the music is the first to break through. In the 1940s, for instance, it was Desi Arnaz and Carmen Miranda who made it cool to be Hispanic.

"What's going to be real hot is the emergence of Latino music," says LaRon Batchelor, a partner at Starpower, which leverages brand power for corporate and entertainment properties. "It always begins with the music."

Ricky Martin, the former Menudo member and *General Hospital* star who stole the Grammy awards show [in 1999] with his Spanglish performance, and whose video, "Livin' La Vida Loca," [was] in the Buzz bin on MTV, [was] becoming the crossover king. [Later in] May, he made the cover of *Time* magazine, when the English version of his album was released and a new duet with Madonna just hit the airwaves.

"Ricky Martin blew everyone away at the Grammys," says Perez of San Francisco, who has worked on Levi's trend advisory panel. "When they scanned the audience, I swore I saw Puff Daddy sitting there, thinking, 'Oh no. What am I going to do now?'"

Martin is just the tip of the iceberg for Latino music, says Batchelor. Party crews in northern California, young Latin trendsetters who deejay, are often brought in by white kids who want to "have a really tight party," says Faura.

Rappers like Big Pun, the first Latino hip hop artist to go platinum, and C-Note, the new boy-group, are on their turntables. Both of Julio Iglesias' young sons are starting to cross over, as is Selena's brother, A.B. Quintanilla, who came out with a hip hop-tinged album. Then there's Marc Anthony, the new Menudo, and Chayanne, who are all appealing not only to Latino teens, but to the Anglos as well.

"I believe it'll catch on," says Batchelor of the trend. "Latino music is a music of passion."

Helping to spread the Latino beat is the variety of musical styles available. If you don't like one style, you're bound to like another that suits your tastes. In Southern California, mariachi, banda, and norteno music rule. Cumbia sounds—like tejano, which uses polka beats and accordion—are hot in Texas. But in Miami, Caribbean salsa is big. New York's clubs play a mix of merengue from the Dominican Republic and rock en espanol, not to mention hip hop.

"It's absolutely happening," says John "Gungie" Rivera, New York's biggest Latin party promoter. "It's just cool now. Common sense tells you with so many Latinos in the world and in the U.S., it was bound to happen."

He not only sees Anglos crowding the dance floors of the Conga Room and the Latin Quarter, but fighting for reservations to restaurants like Patria in New York, Topo La Bamba in Chicago, and Cha Cha Cha in Los Angeles. Latin food has always been popular in the United States, but now it's ultratrendy. Latinos and Latino wannabes alike can be found washing down their fancy $14 lobster-filled empanadas with expensive tequilas and the newest round of imported beers.

In fact, Mexican beer is the fastest-growing import category in the beer industry, says Benitez. "Corona was just leading the way," she says. The newest addition to the market is a beer called Tequiza, which includes the tequila base, agave, and is being marketed by the grandaddy of all brewers, Anheuser-Busch.

Following on the heels of the Latin beat is Latin-influenced fashion. Willie Escobar Montanez, a New York City-based Latino designer, believes that designers like Tommy Hilfiger oversaturated the urban black line. "People are looking for a fresh look from hip hop," he says, "like the Latin look. Our voice is out there now."

Escobar Montanez has added guayabera shirts to his Esco line this year. The boxy, short-sleeved, lightweight shirts were once only popular with old Cuban men because they're extremely comfortable and because of the big breast pocket, perfect for storing cigars. But now kids everywhere, from Miami's South Beach to New York's hip Lower East Side, are sporting the shirts.

Esco isn't the only company making money from the traditional guayabera. In Los Angeles, a young designer named Mario Melendez is making a killing. And down in South Florida, Rene La Villa of Miami Cool Wear has seen his 20-year guayabera business spike by nearly 25 percent in the past two years. Over the Internet, La Villa sells mostly to Anglos. "The guayabera is cool," he says.

Even Donna Karan has added the shirt to her line for women, retailing at a not-so-cool $95.

Other Latin-influenced fashions include baseball shirts with the number 77 printed on them—the former area code for Puerto Rico, explains Escobar Montanez. "The Latin customer immediately identifies with it," he says. "They're not scared of putting something on the garment that says, 'I'm Puerto Rican.' We're no longer refugees."

Straw hats are cropping up in the showrooms of Versace, Dolce and Gabana, and even the Gap. And Che Guevara T-shirts are showing up on college campuses, making the revolutionary the newer, hipper Malcolm X, says one trend watcher.

On the feminine side, embroidered clothes are all the rage. At the national chain retailers Urban Outfitters and Bebe, the Latin theme is big this summer. "I have a friend who works at Bebe who said, 'I think they hired me because I'm Mexican,'" laughs Perez. "I told her, 'Honey, you got that stuff in your closet already.'"

Tighter-fitting, Jennifer Lopez-inspired dresses and pants are also hitting the runways, says Christy Haubegger, president and publisher of *Latina* magazine. "You're seeing different body types, curvier body types that don't look like Kate Moss," she says. Body art like henna tattoos also started with the Latina culture, as did long, brightly colored, airbrushed nails. "Nail art is moving into the Midwest," says Haubegger. "We did that years ago."

Strong eye makeup, darker lined lips, and liquid eyeliner are other fashion trends that are crossing over from the Latina community. "Latinas never stopped using liquid eyeliner," boasts Haubegger. "But now it's like, 'Oh wow! Gwyneth Paltrow is doing it.'"

Hispanic girls spend 60 percent more on make-up than all female teens; 50 percent more on acne products; and more than twice as much on hair products. That's a lot of eyeliner.

Clothes and makeup aren't the only aspects of the culture that white girls are embracing. From the upscale town of Weehawken, New Jersey, to the more laid-back streets of San Francisco, young Anglo girls can be seen doing the Rosie Perez head wag, talking Spanglish, and smoking Newport cigarettes—a Latino brand of choice.

"They talk fast and wag their head," says Perez (Guillermo, not Rosie). Half the time, I'm like, 'Girl, what are you saying?'"

Though some companies, like Anheuser-Busch and DKNY, are already riding the Latino wave, many more are still ignorant of the hip crossover trends, barely even marketing to Latinos themselves, let alone the wannabes, says Faura. They've ignored the fact that the Hispanic population is 30 million strong and is growing four times faster than the general population. Projected Hispanic buying power has increased by 67 percent since 1990, to $356 billion [in 1999].

"Marketers have to understand that the new majority is going to be people of color," says Salzman of Young & Rubicam. "The new minority is going to be your white, 'all-American' kind of kid."

"The sooner the corporations catch wind of it, the better," says Phil Colon, marketing and sales director of *Urban Latino* magazine. "Companies who are behind the curve on this thing might just miss it." A Tommy Hilfiger–like fashion explosion drawing on Latino trends is in America's forecast, says Colon. He believes using the Hispanic community to sell to the wider Anglo audience is inevitable, and a very smart move.

Because the Latin community is so brand loyal, marketing to them pays off in more than just the crossover connection. Once you solidify your support in the Latin community, you have it for years, says Faura. "If you can connect, you've got consumers for life."

However, reaching the target—the young Latin community and their Anglo wannabes—calls for some alternative advertising. "Companies have to start using more nonconventional means," says Colon. "Kids are not hanging out in front of the television. They're not home. They're playing ball or are outside hanging out. Television is not the medium to reach youth. It never was and never will be."

Instead, radio, billboards, stickers, and bus wrapping are both effective and cost-effective, he says.

Faura agrees that marketing to a mass audience using Latino youth culture is not only inevitable but could be hugely successful—more successful than even the recent African American hip hop crossover. "Part of being Hispanic is being authentic and real," says Faura. "There's the soul of it. And if you can capture that in your fashions and in the way you position them, you'll make a bigger splash than Tommy Hilfiger did."

In some ways, it may be harder to market the Latino look than it was the hip hop trend because of the diversity inherent in the Latin culture.

"It's hard to capture the essence of Hispanic teens in one product in terms of clothing and music," explains Angelo Figueroa, editor of the fast-growing *People en Español*, whose circulation rose 25 percent from 1998 to 1999. "Hispanic teens are culturally all very, very different, unlike African American teens in the U.S. who are basically listening to the same kind of music. You have to walk this fine line to make sure it appeals equally to all these groups."

But, he says, branding from Latino trends is not impossible. Just a lot more tricky. Because the population is so huge and is home grown, the ultimate crossover appeal of Latino teen culture could be wider and even more hard hitting than any cultural crossover in the past.

"It'll be harder to do," says Colon, "but the rewards are a lot bigger."

Does Media Sex Influence Young People?

Barrie Gunter

Is there too much sex on TV? When are graphic sexual scenes in film appropriate and when are they gratuitous or pornographic? Is pornography destructive? All of these questions speak to an underlying concern that explicit depictions of sexual relations in media can be harmful. Debates about these questions become especially charged when they are asked with young audiences in mind. The controversies reveal various ways we think about sexual issues like conceptions of virginity, sex with or without love, frequent sex, and gender relations. In this excerpt from his book, *Media Sex: What Are the Issues?*, Barrie Gunter summarizes much of the recent research about possible effects of media sex on teenagers.

Social scientists have long attempted to determine the influence of repeated exposure to sex in television shows, music videos, and movies. Although most studies are not definitive, Gunter concludes that media sex may influence the beliefs and attitudes of young people. Not only sexual scenes, but also talk about sexual relations can instill "sexual scripts." Some of the most common scripts avoid references to the risks and responsibilities associated with sexual relations and therefore teach teens little about sexually transmitted diseases, safe sex, and the risk of pregnancy. However, Gunter notes that media depic-

■

tions that go against this trend can present teens with responsible sexual messages.

Barrie Gunter has written forty books and over two hundred papers, chapters, and reports on a variety of media, management, and psychology topics. He joined the Department of Journalism Studies at the University of Sheffield in 1994 where his principal research interests include children and television and the impact of media violence.

ONE OF THE CONCERNS ABOUT DEPICTION OF sex in the media is the effect that long-term exposure to it might have on viewers. The concern about long-term effects has been focused most especially on young people for whom the mass media represent potentially important sources of learning about social as well as purely sexual relationships. . . .

Risks and Responsibilities in Sexual Relations

One of the biggest concerns about television's depictions of sex—and the same point applies to much sexual content in films and videos as well—is that high-risk sexual behavior is often portrayed. Risky sexual behavior can include sexual practices that increase the likelihood of unwanted pregnancy, especially where this occurs among underage families, or contracting a sexually transmitted disease. Observers in the United States, for example, have noted that risky sexual practices appear to be quite prevalent among American teenagers. Use of contraception among sexually active teenagers is inconsistent and sexual intercourse with multiple partners is not uncommon. These risky sexual behaviors have resulted in a relatively high teen pregnancy rate in the United States compared to other industrialised nations and a steady increase in sexually transmitted disease rates. Full-blown AIDS during adolescence is rare because of the long incubation period. However, more and more health experts believe that many individuals contract the virus during their teen years.

At a time when sexually transmitted diseases are widespread, television's typical depiction of sexual relationships projects a message that appears to run counter to the warnings put about by health education campaigns. Television itself can serve as an incidental sex educator. Although teenagers generally indicate getting information about sex from parents, school, or peers, the media have often been cited as the next most important information source. Indeed, these different sex information sources do not provide consistent advice. There is some concern, for example, that the lessons being taught through formal sex education programs may be undermined by counter examples supplied through peer groups and the media. Avoidance of sexually transmitted diseases and the prevention of their spread can be facilitated by adopting safe-sex practices and by a nonpromiscuous lifestyle. Another social problem that stems from unprotected sex is the increased occurrence of unwanted pregnancies, particularly among teenagers. . . .

At a time when increased sexual responsibility is called for in society, studies of television programming have revealed that appropriate sexual role models have been generally inadequate. Not only has sexual behavior in general increased in prevalence on mainstream television, more importantly, depictions of explicit intercourse have grown in number and frequently take place between partners outside of a permanent or long-term emotional relationship and without any apparent use of protection. Issues of safe sex, sexually transmitted disease, and contraception were rarely addressed on American television between 1979 and 1989. The subject of homosexuality was rarely dealt with. The preponderance of sexual action featured unmarried characters.

Studies About Risk and Responsibility

[D.T.] Lowry and [D.E.] Towles analysed a sample of programs from prime-time network television in the United States in 1987. They were particularly interested in the extent to which sexual portrayals contained references for sexually transmitted disease prevention, unwanted pregnancies, and AIDS. They found 14 references to pregnancy prevention and 18 references to sexually transmitted disease prevention, of which 13 dealt with AIDS, out of a total of 722 sexual incidents coded.

The Planned Parenthood Federation of America conducted another study of network television at about the same time in

1987. This investigation found that references to sex education, sexually transmitted diseases, or abortion were extremely rare, comprising less than a tenth of 1% of sexual incidents.

Research conducted during the mid-1990s by [D.] Kunkel and his colleagues at the University of California, Santa Barbara explored the prevalence, distribution, and character of sexual portrayals on American network and cable television, and paid particular attention to depictions of risks and responsibilities associated with sex.

In a 1-week composite sample of television output comprising 1,170 programs broadcast on 10 television channels, Kunkel et al. found sexual content in 56% of monitored programs, with an average of 3.2 scenes containing sex occurring per hour. More than half the sample of program (54%) contained talk about sex, and just under a quarter (23%) contained sexual behavior. In total, 420 scenes were found with sexual behavior, of which just 45 scenes contained depiction of or reference to risks or negative consequences (2% of all sexual scenes). There were 35 scenes in which reference was made to the use of safe-sex precautions and 13 scenes that depicted waiting for sex until a relationship had developed more fully in other ways. Out of 78 scenes in total that included any reference at all to risks or responsibilities linked to sex, this subject was given substantial emphasis in 41 of these scenes. In the remainder it received little emphasis.

The idea that mainstream television depicts a world of rampant promiscuity characterised by frequent casual couplings between partners who hardly know one another was not upheld by Kunkel et al.'s analysis of mid-1990s American programming. In more than half (53%) of the scenes depicting sexual activity, the characters were in an established relationship. In more than one in four cases (28%), though the characters had not yet established a long-term relationship, they had met before. In only one in ten cases (10%) had they just met.

Despite this character-relationship profile of television's sexual couplings, Kunkel et al. also observed that most television programs that contained scenes of sexual behavior presented no information about the consequences of such behavior for characters. This finding was true both for programs that presented talk about sexual intercourse (63% showed no clear consequences) as well as for those that depicted or strongly implied such behavior (59% showed no clear consequences). When intercourse was the topic of conversation, there was relative balance between the programs that included primarily positive and primarily negative consequences of intercourse (14% positive vs. 16% negative). When intercourse behavior was shown rather than discussed second-hand, there was a much stronger tendency toward positive than negative outcomes (27% vs. 7%).

Out of a total of 456 scenes involving sexual behavior, just 9% were found by Kunkel and his colleagues to contain any mention at all of risk or responsibility, although some of these cases involved jokes or minor references that clearly would not convey a serious message about the topic to viewers. Although this represents only a modest degree of attention to such concerns, it does contrast with their treatment in previous decades. In 1976, only a single scene of 27 involving sexuality (3.7%) addressed any risk or responsibility topic, and that involved a humorous remark about abortion. In 1986, again only a single scene out of 48 (2.1%) was observed, and this comprised a discussion about a possible abortion. In contrast, in 1996, 12 scenes were cataloged in which the use of a condom was mentioned. In five of these cases, it was referred to as protection against AIDS or other sexually transmitted diseases. . . .

Impact on Youngsters

As the content analysis evidence has indicated, television does comprise repetitive sequences of activity related to sexual behavior. Entertainment programming emphasises extramarital sex and displays an apparent disregard for safe sexual practices. Thus, adolescents and teenagers who regularly watch prime-time television are offered a steady mix of marital infidelity, casual sex, the objectification of women, and exploitative relationships.

In a survey of 15- and 16-year-olds in three Michigan cities, more than half had seen the majority of the most popular R-rated movies released between 1982 and 1984 either in cinemas or on videocassette. Compared with prime-time television, these movies had seven times more sexual acts or references, which were depicted more explicitly. The ratio of unmarried to married people engaging in sexual intercourse was 32 to 1. As [B.S.] Greenberg observed, 'What television suggests, movies and videos do.'

A growing number of researchers have investigated the relationship between exposure to sexual media content and adolescents' perceptions, beliefs, values, and sexual behaviors. In general, these studies have shown that there is more evidence for the impact of sexual content on perceptions than on values and behaviors.

Television has, according to some writers, become an important sex educator because of both its frequent, consistent, and realistic portrayals of sexuality and the lack of alternative sources for learning about sexual behavior. Young viewers are provided with frequent lessons in how to look and act sexy. As a consequence, television has become an important sexual socialisation agent. Media depictions of sex can create expectations in the minds of young viewers about the pleasures of sexual activity that contribute towards dissatisfaction with their first sexual experiences. [S.J.] Baran surveyed adolescents about this subject and found that the more highly they evaluated the sexual prowess of television characters, the less satisfied they were with their own initial sexual experiences. This negative correlation between the perceived sexual pleasures obtained by fictional characters on screen and satisfaction with ones own sex life was repeated in a subsequent survey among college students. The degree to which media depictions of sex are perceived as realistic is also important in this context. This, in turn, may be linked to the individuals own sexual experience. Adolescents who were sexually experienced perceived media depictions of sex as less realistic than did virgins, and saw television characters as having less sexual prowess.

In the absence of alternative sources of information, the sexual lessons young viewers derive from television foster an inaccurate image of sex that can lead to unrealistic expectations, frustration, and dissatisfaction. Documenting the specific nature of sexual portrayals on television thus becomes an important step in establishing the reality that influences the perceptions of young viewers. . . .

Mass media are among the sources of information about sex mentioned by teenagers. Teenagers do not all turn to the media for sex information in the same way. For some teenage girls, for example, media depictions of sex are regarded as very useful sources of guidance by which they are intrigued. For others, media sex portrayals are perceived to have little relevance to real life. Indeed, for those girls who are sexually experienced, media depictions of sex may be regarded as overromanticised and as not reflecting their own experience.

Although dispositions towards the media may vary, there is evidence that media sex portrayals may influence young viewers perceptions of sexual activity in reality. Quite apart from any impact that media sex depictions might have on individuals perceptions of their own sex lives, there may be wider effects on social reality perceptions. Regular exposure to televised portrayals of sexual behavior, for instance, has been linked among American teenagers with their perceptions of the frequencies with which those behaviors occur in the real world. [N.L.] Buerkel-Rothfuss and [J.S.] Strouse measured relationships between television viewing patterns and teenagers perceptions of a range of male- and female-linked sexual behaviors.

College students in the high teens were asked to report on their viewing of television in general, and viewing of daytime serials, action-adventure series, evening serial dramas, situation comedies, and high-brow dramas. They were also asked to indicate their views on aspects of male-related behavior (e.g., having an affair, bragging about their sexual experiences, picking up women in bars, fathering illegitimate children, committing rape) and female-related behaviors (e.g., having abortions, talking about sex, feeling guilty after sexual encounters, using sexual favors to achieve goals, and sleeping with multiple partners).

Reported watching of daytime serials or evening serial dramas emerged as good predictors of a wide range of nonerotic sexual perceptions about both males and females. Serial drama viewing predicted perceptions about problems with sex, sex without love, frequent sex, and perceptions about virginity for both males and females. Viewing of MTV was related to perceptions that males and females brag about sex, and consumption of X-rated movies, sex manuals, and MTV were the best predictors of perceptions of the prevalence of erotic sexual behavior. In sum, this study indicated a strong link between the nature of the media selected and the social construction of reality by individuals in their late teens. The real world perceptions that appeared to be influenced were those that involved behaviors portrayed in the media. There was no evidence that perceptions of sexual behavior not depicted in the media were in any way affected by patterns of media exposure.

In a related analysis, [N.L.] Buerkel-Rothfuss, [J.S.] Strouse, [G.] Pettey, and [M.] Shatzer reported a number of relationships between television viewing habits and attitudes to sex. General media consumption was unrelated to such attitudes, but the extent to which young adult males and females watched MTV and television soap operas was linked to holding sexually permissive attitudes. This finding applied to both males and females. Although neither MTV nor television soaps depict explicit sexual content, sexual themes are prevalent in both cases. Even so, the data reported in this analysis were inconclusive as to the direction of causality, and whether the media were causal agents or whether sexually explicit media content was selected by already permissive individuals.

Television Sex and Adolescent Morality Perceptions

Television depictions of sex can provide fictional examples of sexuality, sexual relations, and sexual behavior that teenagers may learn from and even try to emulate. Apart from the social learning through the observation of overt behavioral depictions on screen, television's fictional representations of sexual relationships may convey implicit messages about morality. In other words, are certain types of sexual liaison deemed to be socially or morally acceptable forms of conduct? Content analysis studies of sexual portrayals on television have indicated that sexual relationships often occur outside marriage and even outside of any established emotional relationship. What kinds of lessons might this teach young people who are just becoming sexually active themselves?

[J.] Bryant and [D.] Rockwell reported three experimental studies designed to investigate adolescents' moral judgments about sexual liaisons between characters in popular fictional series broadcast on prime-time U.S. network television. They began by manipulating the television viewing diet of teenage boys and girls, and then had each participant view and evaluate a series of brief video vignettes extracted from television series, some of which depicted sexual behavior. They also examined the mediating influences of family communication style, family value systems and the participants' own viewing styles on their reactions to television's sexual scenes.

Following a forced diet of television programming 3 hours a night for 5 nights, which covered themes of pre-, extra-, or nonmarital sexual relations, young viewers rated the sexual indiscretions or improprieties depicted in video vignettes as less bad compared with same-age peers who had viewed nonsexual material. These effects were much weaker, however, among teenagers who were active and selective viewers, whose families had an open, democratic communication style and well established value systems.

In another examination of the acceptability and value of different televised depictions of sexual conduct, [B.S.] Greenberg, [R.] Linsangan, and [A.] Soderman found that teenage viewers felt that they learned something worthwhile from sexual vignettes about sexuality or about sexual terms. There were variations among different types of sexual scene in terms of how much they were enjoyed or regarded as acceptable for showing on television. Four categories of sexual scene were used in this study, with three scenes adopted in each case: married intercourse, unmarried intercourse, prostitution, and homosexuality. Each scene was rated for enjoyment, realism, humour, sexiness, and suitability for viewing. . . .

The prostitution vignettes were the most enjoyed, and the segments involving intercourse between married couples were the least enjoyed. In the latter case, scenes of intercourse involving married couples, along with such scenes involving unmarried couples, were regarded as the least humorous. Scenes of homosexual activity were rated as the least acceptable, whereas the other three types of sexual conduct were all rated about equally acceptable. The scenes involving unmarried couples engaged in sex were rated as the most sexy scenes overall. . . .

Music Videos

Rock music videos are complex stimuli that combine music with visual content. They can be expected to produce a blend of emotional reactions. Stronger sexual feelings, for instance, might be provoked by very sexy videos than by videos with little or no sexual content. Because music videos are aimed at and consumed primarily by the youth market, and teenagers are regarded as more susceptible to a range of potential social and psychological influences of mass media, there is understandable interest in and even concern about the impact of these videos. The possibility of a link between exposure to music videos and teenage sexual activity was indicated by an American survey that showed that teenagers who exhibited a strong liking for Music Television (MTV) were also more sexually experienced.

In addition to the sex component of rock videos, many have an additional factor—namely their capacity to create physiological arousal through the nature of the music and the volume at which it is played. This factor deserves attention because of the theoretical status of such physical arousal when paired with certain types of content. The theory of excitation transfer, for example, captures the way in which arousal produced by rock music might contribute to wider emotional effects of visual sex or violence within video productions. Within excitation-transfer theory, physiological arousal is related to both the intensity of emotional responses to an event and the strength of its appeal. Thus, both the intensity of the viewers' emotional responses to sexual or violent videos and how appealing viewers find them should be related to the level of arousal or excitation provoked by the sexual or violent images.

Sexual images can become compounded with the music in a music video to enhance its audience appeal. [D.] Zillmann and [N.] Mundorf conducted an experiment in which they edited R-rated sex and violence into a rock music video, either independently or together. Sex was found to increase the appeal of the music, but not so violence. Sex and violence together decreased the music's appeal.

[C.H.] Hansen and [R.D.] Hansen conducted two experiments to examine the effects of sex and violence in rock music videos on viewers' judgments of the appeal of the music and other aspects of the production. In the first study, audience reactions were compared across videos with high, moderate, or low levels of visual sexual content. Visual sex had substantial effects on degree of liking for the music and visual production.

Overall, the visual content of videos judged as high in sexual content was rated as more enjoyable than the visual content of videos judged to have less sexual content. The presence of more sexual content also enhanced overall liking for the music. Viewers also reported feeling more sexy after watching the videos with higher sexual content.

Combining sexual and violent imagery in music videos had the opposite effect of sex on its own. The appeal of music videos declined in the presence of high levels of violence, even though sex was also present. This result confirmed the earlier findings of Zillmann and Mundorf. The latter also observed, however, that the effect of sex was felt mostly in the emotional responses of video viewers to the music being played, rather than to the visual elements of the production. In fact, the presence of sex appeared to diminish the appeal of the visual production among women viewers. Hansen and Hansen, in distinction, found that sex had a strong positive effect on the appeal of both music and visual production. The main difference between these two studies was that Zillmann used R-rated sexual inserts, whereas Hansen and Hansen used milder forms of sex content that had occurred naturally in the original video productions. This difference in methodology, taken together with their respective findings, suggests that the mere presence of sex per se is probably less important to audience reactions to music videos than is the nature of that sexual content.

Comprehension of Media Messages About Sex

Survey investigations of links between verbally reported media consumption habits, perceptions of sex, and self-reports of personal sexual practices among young people can reveal where possible associations exist between such measures, but really only scratch the surface in terms of improving our understanding of the ways in which media messages about sex can influence them.

One important aspect of media influence in this context is the way messages about sex are apprehended and processed by members of the audience. Content analyses of the representation of sex in film and television have identified regular patterns in these portrayals that may present not simply behavioral models to be emulated, but also social scripts that are committed to long-term memory to be invoked to guide behavior in a more general fashion when the right occasions arise. Sexual depictions in the media are not always overt and explicit. Often they are implicit and have to be presumed on the basis of depicted action. It may be more important to understand the extent to which different sexual scripts are being learned from the media than to demonstrate copying of specific incidents shown on screen in relation to establishing how far-reaching media effects on sexual practices can be.

Another relevant factor is that distinct gender-related sexual scripts can be identified. Males traditionally tend to be sexual initiators and females are sexual delimiters. Males are significantly more likely to report that their main motives for sexual intercourse are to have fun and achieve gratification, whereas females report that their main motives are love commitment. The learning that takes place from media depictions of sex, therefore, may take the form of schemas or broad frames of reference to guide thinking about male and female sexuality and to inform sexual conduct in different situations. Factual information about biological matters linked to sex, such as menstruation and the reproductive process, can be conveyed to young viewers by documentary programs. Teenage attitudes toward issues such as premarital sex and birth control have been modified through a specially produced film about birth control. However, there may be wider scripts about sex than can be effectively communicated not just through factual media productions but also through fictional portrayals.

Gender Stereotyping in Board Games for Adolescent Girls

Jennifer Scanlon

As a scholar of gender studies and popular culture, Jennifer Scanlon recognized two topic areas that have been neglected by current research: girls' early adolescence and board games. To fill those gaps, she did her own study combining the two. In her analysis of board games marketed to young teen girls, she outlines several trends. The overwhelming message is for girls to become consumers and make themselves beautiful by using makeup and fashionable clothes. Obtaining a boyfriend—at any cost—is often the central goal for game players. These elements blend into the typical directives young women get from many areas of popular culture: to please others; to learn dependence on males; to view math, science, and computers as male domains; and to define their worth in relation to their beauty. Scanlon also notes the presentation of white, middle-class values as the norm. Her conclusion is that these games are not only ethnocentric, but they promote male, heterosexual, and class privilege as well.

Jennifer Scanlon is a professor of Women's Studies at the State University of New York College at Plattsburgh. She also researches women's magazines, feminist pedagogy, and international feminism.

■

Jennifer Scanlon, "Boys-R-Us: Board Games and the Socialization of Young Adolescent Girls," *Images of the Child*, edited by Harry Eiss. Bowling Green, OH: Bowling Green State University Popular Press, 1994. Copyright © 1994 by Bowling Green State University Popular Press. Reproduced by permission.

IN A 1973 VOLUME OF *MS.* MAGAZINE, LETTY COT-tin Pogrebin introduced a checklist for parents who wanted to buy non-sexist toys for their children. An acceptable toy would be ". . . respectful of the child's intellect and creativity, non-racist, moral in terms of the values it engenders, and nonsexist in the way it is packaged, conceived, and planned for play." One of the board games she recommended was Life, a Milton Bradley product, as it encouraged all players to pursue lives of their own, money of their own, careers of their own.

Now, readers, as the instructions on a game might tell you, advance 20 years. Enter the 1990s, a mall, anytown U.S.A. A parent looking for nonsexist toys for children might, at a Toys-R-Us store, find a few toys and games that Pogrebin would approve of. The game of Life remains popular, and consumers can find numerous trivia games, memory games, and games of skill on the shelves. Unfortunately, however, mall toy stores rely heavily on gender stereotypes for their displays, layout, advertising, and most importantly, products. This paper looks at four gender-specific board games directed at young adolescent girls, examines their messages in light of Pogrebin's now 20-year-old suggestions, and brings to light issues about a much-neglected time period in girls' lives, early adolescence, and a much-neglected area of popular culture or leisure studies, gender-specific games. . . .

Girl Games

Heart-Throb: The Dream Date Game, and Sweet Valley High: Can You Find a Boyfriend in Time for the Big Date? are both produced by Milton Bradley, subsidiary of Hasbro, a company with $410 million in annual sales. Hasbro, with no women on its board of directors [at the time this article was written], produces board games for children and adults as well as a range of other products from teething rings to women's undergarments, baby pacifiers to girls' nightwear. The second two games, Girl Talk: A Game of Truth or Dare, and Girl Talk: Date Line, are produced by Western Publishing Company, which has annual sales of $495 million and produces, among other things, board games for children and adults, gift wrap and novelties, stationery, and books.

Not surprisingly, these four games invite girls to enter the consumer marketplace by encouraging players to use products such as clothing and make-up to enhance their looks. Another game for young adolescent girls, Meet Me at the Mall, more blatantly emphasizes the consumer side of things; players run around the mall, visiting stores like The Gap and Benetton, trying to outbuy the competition. For these four games, though, players must obtain boyfriends rather than consumer goods. Whether one steals one from a friend, wins one through her own matchmaking skills, or reads one into her future, a boyfriend rather than a career or a life remains the player's central goal.

A curious consumer might wonder whether the pursuit of a boyfriend is in fact a typical adolescent girl's primary goal. Unfortunately, researchers have not adequately studied the activities of young adolescent girls. Adolescence and preadolescence have most often been described as periods of conflict, with juvenile delinquency and violence the most frequently covered behaviors. Violence within this group, specifically male violence, receives the most attention from the media as well as from scholars. With this emphasis on delinquency and violence, both defined in male terms, issues in girls' lives are often overlooked. The [1990s] debate over the proposed segregated schooling of African American males, in order to meet their needs, largely ignores the needs of young African American women and exemplifies this trend.

Feminist scholars, however, recently began to take notice. As one puts it, we need to focus on the larger issue of adolescent culture rather than on delinquency and focus on what girls are doing, what their lives are like. Young adolescence may be redefined, in fact, not as violence vs. lack of violence but as peer identity vs. isolation. For girls, this often means close ties to the consumer culture rather than to so-called rituals of resistance. . . .

Gender Messages from Popular Culture

While children repeatedly get these messages at home and in school, they get them from popular culture as well. Widely documented studies of television's influence on gender role socialization reveal the connections between television watching and the likelihood that children and teenagers will have stereotypical beliefs about gender roles. Adolescence heightens sensitivity about gender, and numerous studies demonstrate the extent of gender stereotyping on contemporary television. Males are overrepresented two or three to one in commercial television, and the voice-over in commercials remains male 90 percent of the time. This is significant, of course, as children in the United States watch an average of 40,000 commercials per year. In addition to television, magazines and fiction addressed to preadolescent and adolescent girls stress traditional gender roles, the importance of girls' bodies, and the overwhelming and incessant need to find a boy. Magazines, for example, provide constant reminders that a girl must consciously and continuously cultivate sexual attractiveness, her greatest asset. Magazines, teen formula romance fiction, and other commercial enterprises replay the messages that come, in other forms, through the family and school.

However, unlike family or school, leisure pursuits like reading magazines or playing games do not appear to be coercive. Simply because of this, they demand attention. Associated with freedom, leisure activities for girls often carry heavy ideological messages wrapped in the context of an escape from limits. These activities define girlhood in class-, race-, and behavior-specific ways. Three out of four teen fashion magazines in the United States, with a combined circulation of almost four million, portray young American women as white, very feminine, carefree, boy-crazy virgins. A recent issue of *Teen* featured liposuction and plastic surgery as options for those readers dissatisfied with their bodies. *Sassy*, noted for its initial frank discussions of adolescent sexuality, bent to pressure and omitted much of what made it controversial and, not coincidentally, a favorite among many young women craving honest discussion of their needs. These forms of popular culture, rather than an escape from limitations, provide clear and limited definitions of what it means to be a girl.

Board games, another form of popular culture, are a significant aspect of same-sex play for girls. Girls do not play them with boys, nor do they play them to get boys' attention. As the back covers of the games illustrate, girls play in the company of other girls, often in the privacy of one of their bedrooms. The picture on the back of Heart-Throb is typical: four girls in a bedroom, one of them on the bed, the others lounging on the carpeted floor. The game board sits on the floor, and the background features a telephone, a radio/tape player, and a bowl of popcorn. In fact, three of these four covers show a telephone, a radio/tape player, and popcorn, which is, of course, a low-calorie snack. In this sacred space girls learn to define themselves. Real boys do not invade this very feminine scene, but the idea of boys takes up a good deal of space, as each game encourages girls to think about themselves in relation to boys. By playing these board games, girls learn a central rule: they need boys to complete their self-definition.

Get the Guy

The four games featured here offer young adolescent girls a wide variety of messages, all of them gender specific. From the uniformly "pretty" boxes to the uniform goal of getting a guy, they promote traditional gender role behaviors, emphasize clear messages about race, class, and sexual orientation, and encourage play that is decidedly humdrum if not outright insulting to any young adolescent's intelligence. They clearly fail Letty Pogrebin's test for nonsexist toys, but the way in which they do so and fail young women in the process is worth examining further.

All of these board games promote the idea that the central object in a girl's life is to get a guy. In Sweet Valley High, girls literally race around the school trying to retrieve a boyfriend, a teacher chaperon, and all the accessories needed for a big date. In the process of trying to get it all done first, girls can steal other girls' boyfriends or fight over boyfriends; such behaviors receive rewards.

In Heart-Throb, each player chooses which boy she would like to have ask her out and guesses which boys her competitors will choose. The game pieces include 60 boyfriend cards, each picturing a different boy, and 162 personality cards, which reveal both good and bad qualities of boys. In Girl Talk: Date Line, players match up girl and boy cards they hold in their hands in order to create successful dates. While they travel around the board, trying to set up a date, the players date as well; if they do not secure a date for the imaginary characters they hold in their hands, they themselves must go stag or settle for a blind date.

In Girl Talk: A Game of Truth or Dare, the initial focus seems different. Girls spin a wheel and then must reveal a secret or do a stunt. Many of the stunts are unrelated to getting a boyfriend and include doing situps or sucking a lemon. Others, however, clearly promote the overall gender-enforcing plan and include pretending to put on make-up, calling a boy and telling him a joke, rating your looks from one to ten, or revealing what you would like to change about your looks. Anytime a girl does not complete the required stunt, she must peel off a red zit sticker and wear it on her face for the rest of the game. The game's instructions warn that the zit sticker must be visible: it cannot go under the chin or behind the ear.

The end goal of this game is to collect one of each of the fortune cards, which fit into four categories: Marriage, Children, Career, and Special Moments. However, dependency on boys or men dictates girls' experiences in each of the four categories except Children. Under Marriage, two possible fortunes are "You will marry _____'s boyfriend," or "You will meet your future husband while working together at _____ fast-food restaurant." Under Career, you could receive "After three weeks on your first job as a _____ (profession), you will meet the man that you will eventually marry," or "You will take a job as a carhop just to get a date with a certain boy who drives a _____." Finally, under Special Moments, fortunes include "A tall, dark, and handsome policeman will stop you for speeding and give you a ticket, but will make up for it by asking you for a date," or "While visiting a dude ranch, your horse will bolt and you will be rescued by a ranch hand who looks just like _____ (actor)." In the category of Special Moments, with 24 possible cards, 7 are specifically about boys but only one portrays a girl having a special moment with a girlfriend.

Rigid Gender Roles

Each of these four games portrays girls in strictly feminine terms and boys in strictly masculine terms, with little overlap in traditional definitions. In the Sweet Valley High game, for example, students vote Jessica Most Popular Girl in the school; she is also, not coincidentally, co-captain of the cheerleaders. Elizabeth, Jessica's sister, receives an award for her newspaper column, a gossip column called "Eyes and Ears."

The names used in the Sweet Valley game indicate which girls and boys are popular and which are not. The nerdy and non-masculine boy is called Winston Egbert; Winston prefers feminine activities like talking and being gentle to masculine qualities like playing football and being aloof. The desirable boys in Sweet Valley, Todd Wilkins and Bruce Patman, do masculine things like skiing and driving expensive sports cars.

Names are used as indicators of appropriate levels of feminine or masculine qualities in Girl Talk: Date Line as well. When players land on a date space, they choose two of the character cards in their hand and set them up for a date. When they put the cards together in a microphone machine, girls discover whether or not the date they choreographed went well. The characters Gert and Homer stand out as nerds in appearance, name, and behavior. Both Gert and Homer wear glasses, but none of the many popular characters wear glasses, and the popular people have names like Nicole and Drew, Stephanie and Matt.

In Girl Talk: Date Line, Homer's personality profile reveals that he loves the computer club and collecting bugs but hates sports and school dances. Boys clearly should love sports, including the sport of pursuing girls at dances, whether or not they actually like to dance. Gert, the girl without make-up and hence without much personality, loves Latin and algebra, hates rock music and gym class. Obviously girls should not have academic aspirations. The attributes of the popular people in Girl Talk: Date Line confirm clear rules about what it means to be a girl or boy. Stacie loves talking on the phone and shopping but hates greasy hair and book reports. Tina loves pizza and make-up but hates computers and report cards. Eric, on the other hand, loves tennis and water skiing, hates shopping malls. Matt loves math and football, hates double-dating (wants to be in control?) and haircuts.

In Heart-Throb, girls and boys behave in gender-specific ways in dating. When the players choose which of the boys in the boyfriend cards they would like to date and which they think the other players will choose, it seems that at last girls are making choices. In actuality, though, the rules state that three boys from the boyfriend cards ask the girls first to dance, then to go on a date, then to go steady. The girls must choose from among the three boys. Players have some very limited choices: they can choose which boy they want, but they cannot choose not to accept a dance, a date, or a steady boyfriend. Refusing the advances of all three boys is not an option, regardless of how uninviting they appear in their personality cards.

Race, Class, and Sexuality

These board games clearly promote male privilege, then; they also promote the privileges of race, wealth, and heterosexuality. In the four games, virtually all of the characters are white. In Sweet Valley High, located in California, all of the students are fair-skinned, and the only ones with names that deviate from the most popular or trendy, which include Ken—who does in fact look like Barbie's counterpart—are the names of the nerdy characters, but Winston remains, nevertheless, a Waspy nerd. In Heart-Throb, a game with 60 boyfriend cards, not one of the boys even has an ethnic-sounding name. The only feature that distinguishes a few, and makes them appear perhaps somewhat "different," is the appearance of dark sunglasses. In Girl Talk: Date Line, the trendy names include, for the girls, Danielle, Tina, Allison, and Stephanie, and for the boys, Drew, Trent, Eric, and Brad. This game, interestingly enough, features one African American boy but no African American girls; one wonders who players match him up with for a date.

In addition to the privilege of race, the characters in these games have the privilege of social class. The Sweet Valley High game goes the furthest with this: one character gets rewarded for giving her housekeeper the day off and making her own bed, another for donating a large sum to charity, a third for taking everyone for a ride in her new sports car. In each of the other games, the girls playing the games or the character pieces in the games dress well, have access to income to buy clothing and make-up, and have private space all their own. No apartment living for these girls; they relax in their suburban bedrooms with plush carpet or scoot around town in their very own vehicles.

These board games promote the social control of girls' sexuality as well, with heterosexuality consistently privileged. In three of the four games, the only object is either to secure a boyfriend for oneself or secure one for others. The fourth clearly favors marriage and children as the end goal in life. Each game encourages competition among girls for boys, as girls steal others' boyfriend or find warnings in the instructions, as they do in the Sweet Valley game, that they need to keep an eye on their thieving girlfriends. Girls play these games together, but rather than promoting positive female culture or solidarity, the games teach girls that they cannot trust each other when it comes to their primary life definition: boys. The directions in the Sweet Valley game specify that girls can never have more than one boyfriend at a time; if they pick up a second, they must discard one. In Girl Talk: Date Line, the directions actually state in writing that players should not attempt to match up a girl with a girl or a boy with a boy for a date. According to these games, all girls, even the nerdy ones, can look forward to a shared future. What the games encourage players to share, however, is not the ability to laugh, intelligence, or even stereotypical nurturing qualities; instead, they share a future that must, apparently at any cost, include a man. . . .

Games encourage players to develop particular skills. By encouraging large group play in a variety of settings, many boys' games urge them to achieve success in the world at large. Most girls' games, however, prepare girls for a life in one setting, the home, by emphasizing verbal skills in small groups rather than large, and by taking place indoors. Interestingly enough, although the object of many of the girls' games is to secure a boyfriend, the verbal skills emphasized do not apply to him. In other words, girls learn to talk to each other about boys, but they do not learn to communicate with those boys.

Further research may reveal that girls use these games in subversive as well as stereotypical ways or that, like the latest fashions, these trendy games spend more time in closets than they do in the center of girls' play areas. For the many girls who do play them as designated, however, these sex-stereotyped games promote damaging stereotypes, passive rather than active play, and skills that fall short of young adolescent girls' cognitive abilities. They assume that all girls share a common future of domestic work, subservience to men, and limited life experience. They also further the likelihood of such a future by failing to encourage intellectual growth. In an advice book for girls published in 1936, Mary Brockman wrote that "boys don't want girls to talk too much or try to appear too wise. . . . They want girls to know when to sit back and look interested." Apparently, the lesson lives on. These board games, as much a part of the toy-store world of the 1990s as they were of the 1970s, frame a world of limited possibilities for girls.

4

Sex, Drugs, Violence, and Moral Panic

Why Public Outcry Blames Popular Culture for Corrupting Youth

Ulf Boëthius

Ulf Boëthius is a Swedish scholar of child and youth literature. His historical overview in this excerpt demonstrates how public concern has often condemned popular entertainment as a negative influence on young people. Since ancient Rome, societies have reached moments of heightened anxiety that focus on youth cultures and their perceived connection to moral decline, deviance, and criminality. Modern "moral panics" like these are often played out in the mass media where stereotypes abound and problems become exaggerated for their sensational appeal. Also typical is a rush of opinion from various experts claiming to know appropriate solutions, and, ultimately, some sort of social control may be imposed to "correct" the supposed problem. Moral panics often signal a boundary crisis over new ideas and traditional norms. Anxiety over rapid social change sometimes results in a search for scapegoats. Boëthius introduces helpful social and psychological theories to explain how moral panics arise and why they focus on youth cultures.

■

Ulf Boëthius, "Youth, the Media, and Moral Panics," *Youth Culture in Late Modernity*, edited by Johan Fornas and Goran Bolin. Thousand Oaks, CA: Sage Publications, 1995. Copyright © 1995 by Johan Fornas and Goran Bolin. Reproduced by permission.

POPULAR CULTURE HAS ALMOST ALWAYS BEEN considered a threat to young people. It has been associated with leisure or with the borderline area between family, school or work in which the control of guardians or supervisors has been limited or non-existent. The recurring attacks on popular culture have therefore been lodged primarily by representatives of these spheres: from parents, teachers or others who concern themselves with young people's spiritual and moral upbringing.

A Long History of Concern

As long ago as in early Rome, writers, philosophers and historians were indignant about the people's delight in various forms of entertainment. [Roman satirist] Juvenal's words describing his countrymen's attraction to *panem et circenses*, bread and the circuses, are famous. The theatre was considered especially depraved, 'unmanly' and dangerous, but then people also viewed the sports contests, adopted from Greek culture, as simply immoral or at best a meaningless waste of time. The sporting events were also derided for being a non-Roman, foreign invention. Even the very popular horse races were disdained, for, according to their critics, they prevented people from carrying out more serious and worthwhile activities. Strangely enough, what was accepted in ancient Rome were the bloody gladiator contests which were considered to be educational and to inculcate discipline.

Our few sources do not refer expressly to youth, but that discussion of young people's entertainment was intensive in antiquity is evident from, *inter alia* [among other things] Greek and Roman comedies. [Greek playwright] Aristophanes' *The Clouds* (423 B.C.) is about refractory youth who are drawn to emasculating pleasures and modern ideas, and in the comedies of Plautus and Terence debauched, pleasure-seeking young men and their conflicts with their fathers play a central role.

Medieval cultural powers-that-be seem to have been relatively tolerant of popular culture. However, during the 16th and 17th centuries an intensive and protracted persecution of different forms of popular entertainment began, spearheaded by the church and the aristocracy. Carnivals were accused of fostering sexual laxity, and popular ballads describing various rogues and felons (which were soon available in chapbooks) were condemned for extolling crime and glorifying villains as heroes. In Sweden, 'the father of Swedish poetry', Georg Stiernhielm, warned the aristocratic youth of his time of the dangers of frivolous literature; his famous poem *Hercules* (1658) contains a list of popular novels and other publications which should be avoided. Similar attacks became increasingly common during the subsequent centuries. A peak was reached in Sweden in the mid-19th century when C.F. Bergstedt conducted a lengthy campaign against 'vile literature', and the so-called penny dreadfuls [sensational news sheets] in England were alleged to 'fearfully stimulate the animal propensities of the young, the ardent and the sensual'.

However, not only literary products were attacked. In many countries, other forms of popular entertainment were held to be disreputable: theatre plays, variety, music halls, football matches and dances. The campaigns were largely waged via the mass media, and consequently their intensity and extent increased in tandem with the great expansion of newspapers and magazines in the 19th century.

One of the most intensive campaigns against popular culture in the 19th century took place in the United States. It was initiated in the 1870s by a young erstwhile salesman, Anthony Comstock, who heavily attacked books (particularly the 'dime novels', predecessors of our popular paperbacks, with standardized format, titillating covers and a fixed cheap price), and pictures, photographs and all else considered threatening to the moral health of youth. The base for his activities was the New York Society for the Suppression of Vice, founded in 1872. In 1873, intensive agitation resulted in a law forbidding the postal services to forward material considered obscene or harmful to youth. Comstock (who published the book *Traps for the Young* in 1883) was appointed special state agent with the brief of ensuring that the law was followed—something he did with great zeal during the next four decades. . . .

In the postwar period, comics were considered the greatest threat to youth. Greatly inspired by the American medical examiner Dr Fredric Wertham's *Seduction of the Innocent*, published in 1954, the campaign against comics culminated in the first half of the 1950s. However, the battle was not only waged in the United States but also in a number of European countries—for instance, England, France, Austria, West Germany, Denmark and Sweden. In England and France the campaign resulted in special laws aimed especially at violent comics. . . .

Moral Panics

Researchers have characterized several of these campaigns . . . as 'moral panics'. What is actually meant by a 'moral panic'? The term was launched by the sociologist Stanley Cohen in his book *Folk Devils and Moral Panics. The Creation of Mods and Rockers* (1972/1987), which deals with the public outcry caused by the clash between mods and rockers in England in the mid-1960s. In the first chapter of his book, Cohen reveals what he means by a 'moral panic':

> Societies appear to be subject, every now and then, to periods of moral panic. A condition, episode, person or group of persons emerges to become defined as a threat to societal values and interests; its nature presented in a stylized and stereotypical fashion by the mass media, the moral barricades are manned by editors, bishops, politicians and other right-thinking people; socially accredited experts pronounce their diagnoses and solutions; ways of coping are evolved or (more often) resorted to; the condition then disappears, submerges or deteriorates and becomes more visible.

Cohen adds that as a rule, moral panics are linked with various youth cultures (especially within the working class), whose behaviour is viewed as deviant or criminal.

The mass media play a pivotal part in the process. According to Cohen, they largely create the panic, for instance, by representing the deviation or the factor that triggers it off and their effects in an exaggerated and often directly fallacious way. Cohen's point of view is interactionist; it is not that the assailed social deviation creates the need for measures, but that to an equal degree the social measures create the deviation.

As indicated by the quote above, Cohen is of the opinion that panics always follow a certain pattern. Inspired by various studies of socially deviating behaviour and of people's ways of reacting to catastrophes such as earthquakes or bombs, he distinguishes four phases: 'warning', 'impact', 'inventory' and 'reaction'.

Thus a moral panic develops in the following way. Firstly, there are various warnings which portend the approaching catastrophe. When the catastrophe has occurred (impact) the mass media provide a picture of what has happened (inventory). The reports are warped and exaggerated; the event is depicted as extremely threatening and certain details are given a symbolic character (symbolization). For example, a Vespa [scooter] may be offered as a symbol for the mods, who in turn are associated with youthful felons. The mass media inventory provides the basis for the reaction that follows. Interpretations of what has happened are proffered, and from this interpretive process gradually emerges a sort of system of belief: the mass media present a united front on how one is to understand what has befallen society. The system of belief relates not only to the phenomenon itself but also to its consequences. At the same time, attention is quickened and sensitivity intensified as regards similar deviations (sensitization). A social control culture appears: it may be in part official, managed by authorities and their representatives, but it may also be non-official and consist of meetings, petitions, the formation of groups among the general public. Measures are called for and agitation often succeeds in bringing them about.

At the same time, a culture of exploitation begins to assert itself; different interests try to make use of the phenomenon in question. The exploitation may be purely economic, but it is just as often ideological: indignation and excitement are quite simply used to advance an ideological goal. The consequences of all this, according to Cohen, are that the deviation which prompted the whole thing is reinforced and repeated—until the process finally culminates and ceases, possibly because people believe that the measures taken have had the desired results.

This is how Cohen delineates a moral panic. Thus it does not seem right that, as often happens, a single attack against a phenomenon considered upsetting or shocking is termed a moral panic—even if one may sometimes refer to 'minor panics'. There should be a broad and virtually united opposition to the phenomenon causing the indignation. Further, it should be the mass media that create this opposition—or in any case gives it massive support: the mass media are, as we have said, the driving force. And the course of events should take place rapidly and intensively—following the pattern Cohen outlined. In my opinion, only if these criteria are satisfied can one actually refer to a moral panic. Moral panics should be distinguished from the more protracted moral campaigns which can function as a breeding ground for a panic (and vice versa), but they lack the latter's explosive character and demonstrate other patterns of development. . . .

Media Panics

In Cohen's investigation, a couple of youth groups' deviating behaviour caused the panic. In other cases, the causes have been street assaults (the 'garotting panic' in 1860s England), vicious (black) gangs, drugs in the acid house culture, AIDS or alleged child abuse. The moral panics that have been connected with youth, however, have often been 'media panics'. What has triggered off the alarm has been a new mass medium considered particularly dangerous for youth: dime novels, Nick Carter books, films, jazz music, weekly magazines, comics, videos. Is Cohen's model as valid for media panics as it is for other panics? This is a question that has hardly been asked by researchers; they have simply made use of Cohen's conceptual apparatus however and wherever possible.

A media panic, however, is different in several respects from panics caused by people's actions. The actions of mods and rockers gave the panic that Cohen investigated an element of threatening and provocative unpredictability. In this instance the youths themselves were singled out as 'folk devils' and public outrage was directed against them. But when a new mass medium is turned into a dangerous popular menace and young people are considered its victim, the pattern of reaction becomes different: it rather resembles what happens in natural catastrophes such as earthquakes, cyclones or floods. . . .

It may be added that the accusations directed against the media from one media panic to another are remarkably similar—charges repeatedly levelled over the centuries against popular culture. Ever since the 16th century popular culture has been accused of extolling crime and turning youth into criminals, and even if the culture did not go that far, the morals of the upcoming generation were allegedly shaken. Popular culture is often said to be sexually exciting while simultaneously lowering the moral threshold—as regards violence too. Popular culture is at once dangerous and seductive and attractive; it offers pleasures comparable to those associated with women, drugs or alcohol. It appeals to the emotions and primitive instincts and is sharply contrasted with intellectual, controlled and detached high culture. Popular culture is considered unwholesomely exciting, regardless of whether it is a matter of suspense or excitement, fear or the erotic. According to the most common allegations by its critics, popular culture corrupts the fantasy life of the young and distorts their conception of reality.

Popular culture has been linked with the unbridled and undisciplined masses—not least with women, who were considered equally uncontrolled, irrational and capricious. The perspective of the critics, especially during the 19th century, has been generally male and upper class.

Youth and Media Panics

What are the deeper causes of these recurring moral panics? The question has already been discussed by Cohen, who to begin with indicated historically determined social factors. The panic that broke out because of the conflict between the mods and the rockers had to do with the altered situation of youth after the Second World War. Young people had more money and more free time; and a special youth culture developed. Young people quite simply became more visible than they had been and could therefore be more easily exposed to criticism from adults. At the same time, many working-class youths experienced their situation as unsatisfactory and frustrating, and consequently became more inclined to do things to provoke their elders.

Cohen is doubtless correct here, but it could be added that young people had been visible as a separate category long before the Second World War. Youth began to be distinguished as a separate life phase as early as the late 18th century—soon after the 'discovery' of childhood. In the expanding capitalist society, the bourgeois middle class found it necessary to give their children a better and more fundamental education, and this period of education was gradually prolonged. Youth was also considered to be a life phase in which the erstwhile child was instructed in the norms and ways of thinking of the adult world. It was a necessary period of maturing, during which rebellious contrariness and romantic idealism should be refined into moderation, prudence and control. When the period of youth was over, the young person would have been transformed into an adult individual, prepared to shoulder his or her social responsibility.

The demand for this sort of transitional period between childhood and adulthood was particularly forceful during the latter half of the 19th century when industrialism had its final great surge in western Europe. Middle-class ideologists were supported not only by pedagogues but also by psychologists, who around the turn of the century coined a special term for this phase, 'adolescence'. At this time the middle class also began to try to control and shape working-class youth. Young people and their behaviour were thus focused upon in an entirely different way from before—as were the temptations and dangers they were exposed to. Without doubt, the advent of a special period of youth was an important prerequisite for the moral panics of the last hundred years. However, Cohen broadens the social perspective. These panics are not only anchored in the discovery of 'youth' or young people's gradually altered social situation by the modernization process; they also have a more timeless social function. Cohen (along with the psychoanalyst, Erik H. Erikson) sees moral panics as 'boundary crises', ritual confrontations between socially deviating groups and society's official agents, whose duty it is to define where the boundaries lie between right and wrong and permitted and not permitted. The crises are released by societal changes which rock the foundations of traditional norms.

This point of view greatly resembles that developed by the social anthropologist Mary Douglas in her book *Purity and Danger* (1966), in which she discusses the need to delimit clearly the boundaries between the 'pure' and the 'defiled' found in different cultures. The unclean is something only found in the eye of the beholder, according to Douglas. It appears when a forbidden boundary is transgressed, when the established order of things is disturbed. By branding the disturbing factor as 'filth', one re-establishes order and shows where the temporarily disturbed boundary between allowed and not allowed should be drawn. The boundary may be shifted a bit and drawn in a different place. . . .

As [media researcher] Kirsten Drotner has particularly stressed, media panics are intimately connected with the modernization of society. They tend to crop up during periods when society is undergoing rapid change, when the need to clarify the boundaries between acceptable and unacceptable, between the 'pure' and the 'defiled', is particularly acute. In such situations, the old norms are shaken and the established way of seeing is questioned. Changes create anxiety—which leads to the search for a scapegoat, and then startling, new and magnetic media—often from abroad—are pointed to. American culture in particular has been repeatedly pilloried in media panics, which remarkably often have close links to national or sometimes—as with campaigns against jazz music—out-and-out racist currents. . . .

Why Youth in Particular?

Why is the anxiety about social change linked so particularly to children and youth? Modernization actually affects the whole population. Perhaps, as Drotner suggests, this has to do with the fact that youth comprise a sort of 'avant-garde of consumption'. They pioneer the modern, they fall upon new media and media products. It was primarily young people who consumed the Nick Carter books and comic books, and now they consume films, TV, videos, etc. to a much greater extent than the rest of the population. Obviously, youth are also the most important consumer group as regards computer and TV games.

Hence the young are exposed more than others to the influence of new media. At the same time, we have long held that children and youth are more sensitive and more malleable than others. Youth is a period of strong change when one is wide open to all sorts of influences. Aware of this, guardians and pedagogues have tried to give the young the moral and intellectual education they need to enable them to be right-minded adults, capable of assuming responsibility for the development of society.

In this situation, new media are viewed as a threat—children and youth learn things from them that their guardians consider unsuitable and dangerous. Media panics therefore also have attributes of culture or educational conflicts. That these struggles over the upbringing of youth become so vehement is, in part, because a whole national identity may be thought to be at risk—after all, the next generation comprises the nation's future. . . .

The new media challenge the prevailing cultural values and the authority of the cultural powers-that-be as regards determining what is considered good and bad culture. The media habits and cultural preferences of youth challenge the foundations of norms. It is not surprising that teachers, librarians and other guardians of traditional culture are often in the vanguard of moral panics. Even in the area of culture it may be important to make clear where the line is drawn between the good and the bad—and who has the right to draw it.

At the same time, it is a matter of a struggle over cultural capital. By being curious about the new the young acquire skills that adults lack: young people know more about comics, films, video machines and computers than most adults do. The older generation sometimes experience this as threatening and in response try to put young people in their place.

However, moral panics are also certainly anchored in more general clashes between young and old, between the coming generation and its guardians and supervisors. Judging by the ancient comedies referred to at the beginning of this chapter, such generational conflicts seem always to have existed, at least in our western cultures. Patricia Meyer Spacks [author of *The Adolescent Idea: Myths of Youth and the Adult Imagination*] is of the opinion that conflicts between generations can be as powerful as those between the sexes. Children and youth often feel (as do women) dependent, suppressed and bound. They therefore tend (at least in the middle class) to challenge and provoke the older generation—the generation that possesses social, political, pedagogical and economic power, according to Spacks. The clashes become more clear and conspicuous the further the modernization of society advances and, it may be added, the more youth is separated and prolonged as a special life phase.

Gangs and the Media

Martín Sánchez Jankowski

Images of street gangs in popular culture usually focus on three activities: drugs, sex, and violent crime.
Yet few have examined how this idea of gang life was
developed and perpetuated, creating a mythic prototype in American culture. During his many years of
research on gang life in New York, Boston, and Los
Angeles, Martín Sánchez Jankowski analyzed relationships between gang members and the media. In
this excerpt from his book, *Islands in the Street: Gangs
and American Urban Society*, he examines how the
gang myth is employed by the media and by gangs
themselves to fit each of their purposes. The business
and professional constraints on producing media in
the United States influence how reporters, talk show
hosts, and Hollywood directors deliver stories about
gangs to the public. Jankowski details the common
formats used in media to provide information, understanding, or entertainment. He also documents how
gangs carefully consider their interactions with the
media, and some develop sophisticated strategies to
manipulate stories to their advantage. The mythic
image of gang life is a powerful commodity in our
culture, but it provides little help in seriously ad-
dressing the problems associated with gangs.

THROUGHOUT VARIOUS PERIODS IN AMERICAN
history, gangs have received a great deal of attention from the

■

Martín Sánchez Jankowski, *Islands in the Street: Gangs and American Urban Society.*
Berkeley: University of California Press, 1991. Copyright © 1991 by the Regents of
the University of California. Reproduced by permission.

media. This was especially true during the 1970s and 1980s, when there was not one branch of the media that did not devote a significant amount of time and resources to the topic of gangs. During this period, one could find stories of gangs in newspapers, magazines, radio news shows, television news shows, television documentaries, radio and television talk shows, docu-dramas, and, finally, the movies. In short, the media became the general public's primary source of information about gangs and, as a result, became an important actor in the gang phenomenon. . . .

There are a variety of news mediums that deliver the issue of gangs to the public. Each has assumed one of three formats: reporting, understanding, or entertaining. Each of these formats represents the self-understanding of the media itself, and for each of these formats, the people involved in the media have a somewhat different orientation and relationship with gangs. I shall discuss the nature of these relationships beginning with the format of reporting, moving to the format of understanding, and ending with the format of entertaining. The order of the discussion is substantively relevant because the formats of understanding and entertaining emerge from the information presented in the format of reporting.

The Format of Reporting

In beginning this section on gangs and the media, it is important to emphasize that the news media are in business not only to disseminate information but also to make a profit. This being the case, newspaper editors and radio and television news show producers have both to gather information and to get people interested in reading, listening to and viewing their presentation of it. The news media report about gangs as part of the "routine of journalism." In this endeavor, gangs are reported as events, and in the process they assume a certain image. This image (in the reporting mode) cannot be an accurate representation because limitations of time and space restrict this, but nonetheless the image of gangs provided by most of the news media does accomplish the desired economic goals of creating a general interest in buying a particular newspaper or listening to and viewing a news program.

Information concerning gangs is most often delivered to the

public in newspapers and radio and television news shows under the format of reporting. Newspapers and radio and television news shows all report the current day's "news." Of course, rarely does a story about gangs become newsworthy unless it has something sensational to it. After all, it is the nature of the media that they cannot include *all* the news (even if the *New York Times* proclaims "All the News That's Fit to Print") because time and space are limited. This means that gangs must provide enough interest to merit a specific amount of space and time, which usually means that the story must involve violence and/or crime. The more violent the crime, the more likely it is that it will be included in the nightly news. Hence, it is the public's interest in violence that is being addressed, not simply the occurrence of a crime in the city. News shows (as well as newspapers) need a significant number of "interest-generating" events to hook listeners/readers into their respective mediums. The violence and crime associated with gangs are perfect topics for this because they accommodate the public's interest in violent acts, while avoiding many of the technical problems that reporters encounter with other stories related to violent crime. For example, all reporters recount what they consider to be the important events of the day, and they do so in a manner that presents these events as verified facts. Yet in most cases involving gangs, the suggestion that the events being reported are verified facts is somewhat deceptive. In all three [of my] cities studies (Los Angeles, New York, and Boston), an inordinate number of violent events were reported as "gang-related" crimes. In a significant number of these cases, the public was presented with an event as "truth" despite the fact that the nature of the event was not substantiated. When experts (usually the police) were asked to comment on an incident, they most often used guarded language, such as "we believe this to be a gang-related crime." In such cases, the news industry is able to report an interest-generating crime (event) without having to identify a specific person or group of persons who committed it. In addition, such stories about gang violence allow a reporter (and the news establishment) to identify a perpetrator (the gang) without having to worry that they may have impaired the criminal justice process. In essence a story about gangs is perfect. It creates reader-listener interest with few journalistic liabilities. . . .

The Format of Providing Understanding

Given that reporters have limited contact with gang members, it is not surprising that the news-reporting mode of the media offers the public little in-depth information (and sometimes even inaccurate information) on gangs. Nonetheless, the gang-related story serves a useful purpose in that it provides a hook to secure readers and viewers. After all, TV producers are aware of the impact of "audience flow," the phenomenon where someone chooses to continue to watch a particular station because of liking the previous show, and they try to take advantage of this by producing an interesting and informative news program. Editors of newspapers and magazines attempt to provide a hook by producing interest-generating headlines, lead stories, and covers.

These same editors and producers are aware of the limitations of the news-reporting approach, but they know that if they do a good job with the news, the audience's appetite for additional information will be stimulated. The reporting approach thus provides editors and producers with an opportunity to generate an interest that can later be capitalized on by developing presentations such as feature articles, segments in TV magazine shows, and documentaries to provide more understanding of an event reported in limited fashion in the daily news.

The second format in which the topic of gangs is presented to the public is that which I have labeled understanding. Within this format, the goal is to provide a greater understanding of the nature of gangs. For television, Edward R. Murrow's CBS documentary "Who Killed Michael Farmer?" is the classic on gangs and is often used in college media courses as the prototype of how to do a documentary. In this documentary, Murrow takes an incident reported in the news (as an event) and provides a deeper analysis in an attempt to explain the events that led to the death of a crippled young man at the hands of a street gang in the Bronx. In so doing, he sought to provide the public with a general understanding of gangs in urban America. The show aired in the 1950s, but its format has been, to a greater or lesser extent, utilized by subsequent reporters doing documentaries on gangs ever since.

If one were to compare Murrow's "Who Killed Michael

Farmer?" with Dan Medina's "Our Children: The Next Generation," Dan Rather's "48 Hours: On Gang Street," or Tyne Daly's "Not My Kid" (all done in 1989), one would discover that they all used similar techniques to format their shows. Each started with a recent event and then proceeded to weave information on related events into a general story about gangs. In the case of Murrow, the event was the death of Michael Farmer; for Dan Medina and Dan Rather, it was the multiple deaths that have resulted from gang conflict in Los Angeles. Each of these events was reported on the nightly news, and each was used as a core around which a story could be developed. Those who viewed each of these documentaries were presented with programs that alternated between focusing on the core event(s) and those related to specific gang members. All the programs tried to present an interesting and moving story. For Murrow, the task was somewhat different, in that he was focusing on one gang and one event, whereas for Medina and Rather the focus was on multiple acts committed by several gangs.

In Murrow's documentary, the story begins with the murder of Michael Farmer and then proceeds to weave in those events that occurred prior to Farmer's death in an effort to inform the audience more fully about its cause. The documentary is quite compelling because as it moves toward the actions that ultimately would kill Michael Farmer and badly injure his friend, it intersperses the personal histories of his assailants and the attitudes of Michael Farmer's parents. It thus includes both emotion and suspense in the telling of the story. Yet, although it is masterfully done, it has serious shortcomings where gangs are concerned. The show starts with the death of Michael Farmer at the hands of a number of gang members. It addresses the question of who killed Michael Farmer and proceeds to present information on the individuals involved in the murder. The information provides insights into some of the circumstances that influenced the perpetrators of the crime, but offers almost nothing about the nature of the gang itself. What is presented about the gang is that Michael Farmer was the innocent victim of a gang war. However, the program offers little information concerning gang organization and behavior. Even when Murrow answers the question "Who Killed Michael Farmer?"

at the end of the program, his answer is that society killed him by neglecting the horrible socioeconomic conditions that lead boys to form groups that attack people. In a sense, the answer to the question reinforces the imagery of the gang as a group of individuals resembling a pack of hungry predatory animals, such as wolves or coyotes. Thus, because the viewer is not given any in-depth understanding of gangs, she or he has no way of comprehending the relationship between the gang and the crime. The result is that the documentary acts to reinforce another American myth—the gang. . . .

The Format of Entertainment

Television talk shows and the movies take the public's interest in gangs one step further. Rather than attempting to inform the public about gangs, these two mediums attempt to entertain the public with the topic of gangs. Although each differs in the manner in which it entertains, both produce similar consequences.

Television talk shows such as "Geraldo," "The Phil Donahue Show," and "The Oprah Winfrey Show" present/sell themselves as programs that not only inform people on various topics, but also depict the "human side" of stories because they emphasize people's feelings about issues. For such programs, it is imperative that they maintain high ratings or they will be discontinued. Therefore, all focus on those topics believed to be the most stimulating. They must use their topics to sell the event (show). Therefore, their particular format is constructed to produce this effect.

The topic of gangs is one that can stimulate viewer interest, especially if it is sensationalized. Talk shows begin with the host setting the focus for the topic and the tone of the show. In order to do this, the most popular images concerning the topic are used. In relation to gangs, each of the hosts begins with an introductory statement in which the inflection and tone sensationalizes the gang as an important problem facing America. This is done by describing the violent incidents associated with gangs, reporting the experts' estimates of the magnitude of the problem, and stressing the seriousness of the situation. Usually this means that incidents involving violent crime are reported along with the number of innocent people injured, especially the number of innocent people who reside outside gang neighborhoods.

Since these programs present a different topic each day (five days a week), there is little time to do a substantial amount of research on any one topic. To compensate for this, the program offers the audience in the studio and at home a panel of so-called "experts" in the field who are called upon to comment on various statements made in the program. The guests are manipulated by the host for the most dramatic effect. The statements by the guests are severely limited by the host to only a few brief paragraphs and are ultimately used to establish the groundwork (substance) for what is the essence of the program: the various interactions of the host, the guests, the audience in the studio, and the audience at home. In the shows on gangs, a number of obvious questions were asked, such as, Why do young kids join gangs? Why do they act violently? What can be done about them? It is next to impossible to give an informed answer to these questions in a thirty-minute program in which there are a number of guests with varying degrees of expertise and opinions on each of the subjects.

The host interacts with the guests, drawing out different and opposing positions on the topic. The objective appears to be to initiate conflict among all the participants (apparently because it is believed that conflict is capable of arousing viewer interest) and to maintain the show's intensity by stimulating interaction among the guests, between the audiences in the studio and at home, and between the guests and the members of the audiences. The main function of the host is to act as provocateur and to incite verbal combat between the different groups involved in the show. It is apparent that producers believe that if they can get the audience in the studio worked up, they can excite the audience at home. Although the general strategy of the shows I reviewed produced lively discussions on gangs, there was little understanding provided of the gang phenomenon. Of course, the format of the show, and its primary intent, was not to provide understanding, but to use the topic of gangs to sell the spectacle of the participants' interactions. Ultimately, these programs provide entertainment and in the process reinforce the public image of gangs and the gang problem.

Gangs in Movies

Motion pictures are the other medium in which gangs are utilized to entertain people. Although there are a number of pictures in which gangs are the focus, three of the more memorable are *West Side Story*, *The Warriors*, and *Colors*. Each of these movies depicts the gang in a different era, with *West Side Story* focusing on the 1950s, *The Warriors* on the 1970s, and *Colors* on the 1980s. Yet despite the fact that they are obviously bound by their respective time frames, they are also remarkably similar in the way they depict gangs and the people with whom gang members intimately interact.

Let us begin with Hollywood's depiction of gangs. Each movie mentioned above depicts gangs as composed of poor or working-class males who lack the skills and desire to be upwardly mobile and productive citizens. Essentially, they are not only "losers" but "losers" who are also primitive and brutally violent. Their values are painted as both an anathema to the values held by the society as a whole and a threat to them (society's values).

Those who are intimate associates of gangs are likewise characterized in a negative manner. The parents of gang members are presented as individuals who do not care and/or are negligent in their parental responsibilities. However, while most people closely associated with gang members are presented in a negative light, none are represented worse than the women with whom they interact. Gang movies, by requiring a love/sex angle, make gangs revolve around sex in a way that is both sexist and racist, and this distorts their picture of gang behavior. In each of the movies on gangs, the women whom gang members interact with (regardless of whether they are girlfriends, lovers, or acquaintances) are portrayed as having loose morals. They are willing either to engage in open, nonmarital sex or to sell sex (prostitution), or they are alcoholics and/or drug addicts. This imagery is particularly provocative because most of the movies focus on nonwhite gangs in nonwhite neighborhoods. One need only compare the portrayal of nonwhite women and white police officers in *Colors* with those in *Fort Apache, The Bronx*, an earlier film that focused on life in an extremely depressed community. In each of these films, all the nonwhite women but one are portrayed as being immoral and/or irresponsible in some significant way. In both films, the one nonwhite woman introduced as being different from the rest is also portrayed as having escaped the corrupting influences of the others in her community. One is a Puerto Rican nurse (in *Fort Apache*) and the other is a Mexican who sells food from a take-out stand (in *Colors*). Of course, in each movie the white police officer (Paul Newman in *Fort Apache* and Sean Penn in *Colors*) falls in love with the "different" woman. Yet later in each film, we find out that neither woman is "good" at all; it has just been a masquerade. The Puerto Rican nurse is a heroin addict and the Mexican waitress is actually a slut who hangs out with her barrio gang. Both are not only portrayed as dishonest with their white boyfriends but betray them in ways the dominant society sees as morally reprehensible. Both women have been offered a way out of the slum and the immoral life that pervades it, yet both are depicted as incapable of seizing the opportunity. The Puerto Rican nurse refuses to give up heroin and dies from an overdose, and the Mexican waitress refuses to continue to date Sean Penn, who later finds her at a gang party having sex, not only with a gang member (his symbolic enemy), but with the only African-American member of a Mexican gang! The symbolic message is quite striking here. Having sex with a Mexican gang member would be immoral enough, but having it with the only African-American in the gang is the ultimate in betrayal. . . .

The Gang and the Media: Hamming It Up for Glory and Gain

Gangs are not so awestruck by the media and the prospects of being written or talked about that they unequivocally give reporters whatever information they want. They are willing to give information, but only on their own terms. They assume this position because they are suspicious of reporters (part of their defiant individualist characters) and conscious of the fact that information about them is in high demand and therefore has value. All the gangs studied realized that the media were consistently interested in doing stories about them, provided the information imparted was novel. Therefore, they all offered information, but they regulated its flow in terms of both depth (degree of intimacy) and quantity. . . .

In the more than ten years of my research, I never observed gangs receiving money from the media for their cooperation in giving information. At no point did I ever observe any member of the media even offering money. The obvious questions are: (1) If gangs do not receive any money, what do they get for their cooperation with the media? and (2) Why do gangs believe it is important to have some policy guiding their interaction with media?

To answer the first question, we can begin by stating that gangs are able to secure a number of organizational and personal advantages (albeit modest) from media coverage. First, media coverage can help them recruit new members. A gang that has been given media exposure will often be able to start another branch of their organization in another section of the city because the publicity has created interest among enough young males who live there. . . .

The second advantage that gangs receive from media coverage is advertisement for business. They want the television coverage to depict them as being in control of a specified territory and willing to use physical coercion if necessary. This has helped them in their protection business. When they approach a new business with the proposition of providing protection, being in the news sometimes helps them secure the new client. Of fifty-three small business people I interviewed after they had agreed to have a gang protect their businesses, 30 percent (sixteen) said that they had been influenced (intimidated) by stories about that gang in the media. . . .

Gangs and the media have established a relationship that ultimately helps both to maintain a status position within society. Together they have reinforced the folkloric myth of gangs within American culture. Of course, it is important to emphasize that this myth is one that carries a negative image. It is one that has demonic qualities. For gangs ultimately are depicted as not only physically threatening average, law-abiding citizens, but also as undermining the morals and values of the society as a whole. They are carriers of moral disease within the social body. It is this image, an image based on personal and group fear, that has excited the interest of the general public; and it is this image that has reinforced the status of gangs within American culture.

Although the media present gangs as demonic, the organs of public opinion actually participate with gangs in a mutually beneficial exchange relationship that does not contribute to the elimination of gangs. Gangs in the media constitute a sustaining cultural myth, a myth predicated on shared cultural images and distortions of actual social reality. The media distort gang operations in several ways. First, the media emphasize the violence associated with gangs and the violent nature of gang members; but while violence does occur involving gang members, it is less central to gangs (or their members) than the media would lead one to believe. Second, gangs are not exclusively a nonwhite phenomenon, as the media's portrayal would suggest. Although poor nonwhite communities have produced the largest number of gangs, poor white communities have had gangs in the past and continue to produce gangs. This study reports on Irish gangs, but there are, for example, Italian and Appalachian white gangs as well. Third, poor communities are no more socially disorganized than other communities and no less capable of establishing civic control. Finally, the depiction of promiscuous nonwhite women entrapping upright white men has a long history in the American imagination and speaks more to white racial and sexual fantasies than to anything that happens in gangs. The findings in this study suggest that gangs are a commodity, whose depiction produces value for those who work in the media industry. Because the general public is interested in understanding gangs, a story that exploits that interest can produce revenues for the media business and money, mobility, status, and power for the reporters involved. This is why reporters want the so-called "experts on gangs" to tell the truth, but want them to do so within the context of images that create interest among the general public: sex, drugs, crime, and violence. As with the first gangs, the western outlaws, this folkloric myth of gangs is a distorted picture of them.

Sex and Sexism in Teen Music and Music Videos

Jeffrey Jensen Arnett

Jeffrey Jensen Arnett's research focuses on popular music and adolescence, as his two recent books attest: *Metalheads: Heavy Metal Music and Adolescent Alienation* (1996) and *Adolescence and Emerging Adulthood: A Cultural Approach* (2001). In this essay, he combines his interests to examine how sexuality is portrayed in songs and music videos favored by teens. Many studies have shown that teenagers spend more time listening to music than they do watching television. However, in comparison, little research has been done to learn more about the relationship between music and attitudes toward sex. Arnett acknowledges that teens enjoy music for entertainment, yet their listening habits also influence identity formation and coping strategies, especially in relation to gender issues and sexuality. Like others in this collection, he emphasizes the need for research about what teens themselves believe about the subject under study—in this case, the role of music in their lives.

POPULAR MUSIC AND SEX HAVE GONE TOGETHER like a horse and carriage ever since the days of the horse and carriage. Early in the 20th century, jazz and blues were noted (and vehemently criticized) for the sexual intensity of both their

■

Jeffrey Jensen Arnett, "The Sounds of Sex: Sex in Teens' Music and Music Videos," *Sexual Teens, Sexual Media: Investigating Media's Influence on Adolescent Sexuality*, edited by Jane D. Brown, Jeanne R. Steele, and Kim Walsh-Childers. Mahwah, NJ: Lawrence Erlbaum Associates, 2002. Copyright © 2002 by Lawrence Erlbaum Associates, Inc. Reproduced by permission.

music and lyrics. ("You can't keep a good man down," Mamie Smith sang in an early blues song, and her meaning was not lost on her listeners.) In the 1950s, jazz and blues gave way to rock and roll, and the explosive sexuality of Elvis, Little Richard, and others. From the 1960s to the present, sexual themes have increasingly permeated popular music, in genres ranging from ballads to rock to rap. The portrayal of sexuality in popular music has become less subtle, more explicit; by the 1980s, George Michael was singing "I Want Your Sex," and we had moved a long way from the subtlety and playfulness of jazz and blues.

Popular music has always been most popular among the young, who are attracted to the sexual intensity of both the music and the lyrics. Today's teens spend a considerable amount of their time immersed in popular music. In fact, listening to music is their top activity outside of school. In one survey, 92% of teens (aged 14 to 17) said they had listened to music on the radio during the previous day; 88% had listened to recorded music. Integrating a variety of studies, [P.G.] Christenson and [O.F.] Roberts concluded that during their high school years, American teens listen to music about 3 to 4 hours per day, on average (compared to 2 to 3 hours per day for TV watching). Music is frequently a secondary activity, a background to some other primary activity, often one that has sexual overtones: dancing, parties, going to nightclubs or other social events. But teens listen to music in many other contexts as well. For example, over half of teens listen to music while doing homework.

In this [viewpoint] we begin by looking at portrayals of sexuality in songs and music videos popular among teens. Then we present a theoretical framework for understanding teens' uses of sexually themed songs and videos. Finally, we suggest directions for future research, advocating a more teen-centered approach.

Sexuality in Songs

Themes of the songs most popular with teens are diverse, ranging from social and political issues to loneliness and alienation. However, for many decades the most common themes in popular songs have been related to sexuality: love, romance, gender, and sex itself. Various content analyses have shown that from the 1940s to the present, between 70% to 90% of popular songs have contained themes related to sexuality. In one analysis, [E.D.] Edwards classified the lyrics in popular songs from 1980 to 1989, using the top 20 singles from each year. (Because songs in genres such as heavy metal and rap tend to be purchased in albums rather than as singles, these genres are underrepresented in this analysis as in most other content analyses). Phrases in songs with themes related to sexuality were classified as optimistic or pessimistic and as physical or emotional. Eighty-five percent of the songs were found to have references to sexuality, and sexuality was the dominant theme in 72%. Sixty-seven percent of the songs had one or more optimistic phrases, but 77% had one or more pessimistic phrases. Phrases were evenly balanced between physical and emotional aspects of sexuality. Lyrics rarely reflected any hesitancy about entering into a sexual relationship, despite the threat of AIDS and other sexually transmitted diseases (STDs). As Edwards dryly noted, "there was more concern about broken hearts than about disease or pregnancy".

Although songs with themes of sexuality have been consistently popular with teens over the decades, there has been a steady increase since the 1950s in the explicitness of the sexual lyrics in popular songs. Content analyses indicate that there has been a trend toward emphasizing the more physical aspects of sexuality, and less emphasis on its emotional aspects. However, casual sex tends to be portrayed as resulting in unhappiness. Emotional themes remain frequent in current songs. Both males and females are often portrayed in popular songs as fools for love—needy, vulnerable, anxious, sad. "Show me how you want it to be," Britney Spears pleads in a recent example of this, her "Baby One More Time"; "My loneliness is killing me."

Although emotional neediness is more commonly attributed to females than males in popular songs, this appears to have become less true over time. In a content analysis of songs from 1945 to 1976, [V.] Cooper found that over this period females in popular songs were portrayed less often as dependent and submissive, more often as powerful. However, as they became more powerful they also became portrayed more often as threatening, evil—dangerous seductresses. A recent example of this can be found in Ricky Martin's "Livin' la Vida Loca"; "Once you get a taste of her you'll never be the same/She will make you go insane."

Sexuality in Music Videos

Music videos have become highly popular among teens since the early 1980s, especially among younger teens. Teens watch music videos for about 15 to 30 minutes per day, on average. Although this is much lower than the 3 to 4 hours a day typical among teens for music listening more generally, watching videos tends to be a primary rather than a secondary activity. The proportion of music videos with sexual imagery varies by genre, from about 50% of pop and rap videos to just 8% of heavy metal videos.

One of the most striking features of music videos is the sharp demarcation of gender roles, especially in relation to sexuality. One analysis of 1,000 music video characters found that males are more often depicted as adventurous, aggressive, and dominant; females, in contrast, are more often depicted as affectionate, fearful, and nurturing. Another analysis, comparing videos in different musical genres, found that rap videos were especially likely to be sexist, with females depicted as sexual objects.

Although music videos are fairly diverse in themes and scenes, if there is such a thing as a typical music video it features one or more men performing while beautiful, scantily clad young women dance and writhe lasciviously. Often the men dance, too, but the women always have fewer clothes on. The women are mostly just props; not characters, not even people, really. They appear for a fraction of a second, long enough to shake their butts a couple of times, then the camera moves on.

A prime example of this is in the video for Ricky Martin's "Livin' la Vida Loca." Throughout the video, the mostly naked women shake and dance sexily. Ricky dances too, but he never shows any skin. This double standard reaches absurd proportions in "La Vida Loca." The song contains the line "She'll make you take your clothes off and go dancing in the rain," but when this line is sung, Ricky is depicted dancing in the rain with all his clothes on, while a circle of women dancing around him strip theirs off.

Why doesn't Ricky take at least some of his clothes off? Why are women depicted in so much more sexually alluring ways than men in music videos? For the same reason that there are more strip clubs featuring naked female dancers than naked male dancers, and more pornographic magazines featuring naked females than naked males: Because it is more acceptable to reduce females to their sexuality than to reduce males to their sexuality. The sexual double standard of music videos reflects the sexual double standard of the larger society. Ricky does not take his clothes off—not because he would not be even more sexually alluring if he did, but because he would never submit to the indignity of being depicted as a sexual object. For women, however, such indignity is expected to be a standard part of their gender role.

Although the depictions of sexuality in "La Vida Loca" are typical, music videos are diverse, and there are important exceptions. One of the most interesting of these exceptions is a video by TLC for their song "Unpretty." In contrast to most other videos, which implicitly confirm gender stereotypes, "Unpretty" directly challenges the cultural pressures that young women face with regard to sexuality. In the primary story line, a young woman considers breast enlargement at the urging of her boyfriend. She is shown going to a cosmetic surgery clinic and being prepared for surgery, but at the last minute she tears off the hospital gown and flees. Next she is shown with her boyfriend, angrily rejecting him for coercing her into the surgery. In a secondary story line, a plump adolescent girl is shown in her bedroom gazing at the thin magazine models she has pasted on her wall. She cuts out a picture of her own face and tapes it onto the body of one of the models, clearly aspiring to look like them. At the end of the video, however, she tears the models down off her walls as she decides to accept herself for what she is. Thus, in both story lines young women are shown rejecting the cultural influences that make them feel "so damned unpretty."

Another striking feature of music videos is that the visual images are often much sexier than the music. This is partly because visual depictions of sex are inherently more arousing than auditory depictions of sex, but also because the videos sometimes take a nonsexual song and make it highly sexual. One example of this is Lenny Kravitz's "Fly Away." The lyrics of the song have nothing to do with sex ("I want to get away/I want to fly away/Yeah, yeah, yeah."). The video, however, shows a club scene with Kravitz and his band playing the song as young people—especially the de rigueur scantily clad young women—dance lasciviously. At one point, one of the young women even takes her shirt off, although her bare breasts are censored by blurring them.

The reason for sexualizing music videos even when the topic of the song is nonsexual is not hard to discern: Sex sells, in music videos as elsewhere. Studies of college students have found that they tend to rate videos with sexual imagery higher than other videos. High school students, especially males, respond to sexually explicit videos even more favorably than do college students.

Teens' Perceptions of Sexuality in Songs and Music Videos

What do teens make of the sexual images in songs and music videos? To what extent do they perceive as sexual the themes and scenes that academics code as sexual in content analyses? Studies on this topic concur that young people interpret song lyrics and music video imagery differently, based on a variety of factors, including social class, ethnicity, gender, interests, and experiences. The most important factor influencing their interpretations is age. In particular, preadolescent and early adolescent children tend to be highly literal in their interpretations, so that they often miss the implied sexuality in the song. For example, Greenfield et al. (1987) examined responses to song lyrics and music videos among college students as well as children in the 4th, 8th, and 12th grades. The fourth and eighth graders often missed the meaning of the lyrics, especially when the lyrics involved sexuality. Reviewing studies of age differences in responses to song lyrics and music videos, Christenson and Roberts (1998) concluded that for children and early adolescents, "their ignorance helps preserve their innocence. . . . it is not so much a case of 'you are what you hear' as 'you hear what you are.'"

Given that young people spend a great deal of their free time listening to music, that their music has a high degree of sexual content, and that sexuality is a key area of development during adolescence, it is surprising that there has not been more research devoted to the relation between music and sexuality in adolescence. Far more research has been conducted on adolescents and television, although adolescents spend more time listening to music than watching TV and they watch less TV than persons in any other stage of life.

Furthermore, a substantial proportion of research on adolescents and music has been conducted using study designs of questionable validity. The most common design for studies in this area involves having college students respond to songs or music videos in a laboratory situation, in return for credit for a psychology course. The problems with this approach are many, including the facts that (a) college students are too different developmentally from adolescents for findings to be generalizable from one group to the other; (b) college students are not representative even of their age-group; and (c) college students volunteering to take part in a study for course credit are not representative even of other college students. More importantly, the studies are frequently conducted in university classrooms or laboratories, and as a consequence may lack contextual validity. That is, it is difficult to assume that watching preselected music videos in a professor's lab or a university classroom is the same as watching music videos with friends, family, in the dorm, at a bar, or alone.

This design also ignores that adolescents make choices of which music and music videos to consume, based on their own preferences. A researcher might show music videos containing images of sexual violence to 20 subjects, and claim to find an effect of the music videos on the respondents' attitudes about violence toward women, when in reality only 2 of the 20 would ever watch such music videos of their own volition. The effects of the videos on those 2 respondents may be different from the effects on the other 18, yet this would not be apparent in the data analysis or the report of the results. The data from the only 2 individuals who would actually choose to watch these music videos would be lost in the noise from the 18 who would never be exposed to them in real life. This design treats people as blank slates, having no important differences among them that would lead them to make different choices about their music consumption or that would cause them to respond in different ways to the music and music videos that they do consume.

We believe that research on sex and teens' music would benefit from the application of a theoretical framework that focuses on what young people themselves say about the meanings of the music. Specifically, we propose a model based on the uses and gratifications approach to media research. At the heart of this approach is the idea that people make choices about the media they consume, and that their choices are guided by the uses they believe they can make of media and the gratifications they gain from their media experiences. Rather than viewing people as passive and easily manipulated targets of media, the uses and gratifications approach views them as active agents who determine to a large extent the media to which they are exposed, through the choices they make in an environment in which a vast range of media content is available.

With respect to teens, music, and sex, the uses and gratifications approach suggests the questions: What uses do teens make of songs and music videos with sexual themes, and what gratifications do they gain from them? We address this question, using a framework that has been employed previously as a general framework for understanding adolescents' uses of media. Here, we apply it specifically to adolescents' uses of songs and music videos with sexual themes, using current examples for illustration. The three uses considered are entertainment, identity formation, and coping. These three uses are not meant to be exhaustive, but to be considered examples of the uses that teens may make of sexually themed songs and music videos.

Entertainment

Adolescents use sexually themed songs and music videos as daily entertainment, as a way of pleasantly passing the time. Music provides an almost constant background to their activities outside of school, and most of the music they like best contains sexual themes. They listen to music while doing their homework, while driving a car, and while walking or jogging, but especially in contexts where the focus is on leisure; no teen party would be complete without music. For music videos, too, teens state that one of their top reasons for watching them is entertainment.

A substantial proportion of the songs and music videos that appeal to teens have entertainment as their evident aim. The songs and music videos of Madonna have provided good examples of this over the years. Neither the lyrics nor the music in her songs are very distinctive or original. The topics tend to be sexual—dancing, flirting, boys and girls meeting and pairing up and parting again—all long-standing, well-worn themes of popular music; the lyrics are also laden with clichés. But to teens, the appeal of the songs may be precisely the fact that they are so predictable and demand so little from the listener. They are like a tasty confection, easy to consume and quickly forgotten, but pleasant to experience for the moment—to dance to, to tap your foot to, to sing along with, to fantasize with.

Many music videos have elaborate dance routines that add to their entertainment value. Recent videos by Britney Spears, Jennifer Lopez, and Christina Aguilera are in this vein. For example, in "Baby One More Time" Britney Spears and her supporting cast engage in elaborate synchronized dance routines throughout the video. The setting is a high school, and they are shown dancing mainly in the hall and the gymnasium. The dancing is mildly provocative, and Britney is dressed in a revealing outfit. The lyrics of the song are actually rather somber and brooding, but the music and the dancing change the spirit of the video to pure entertainment, a celebration of youthful vigor and sexuality.

Identity Formation

Identity formation has long been viewed as one of the key developmental challenges of adolescence. It consists of gaining a clear sense of one's interests, needs, desires, and abilities with respect to love, work, and beliefs. With respect to love, it includes both developing a sense of one's sexuality and developing a gender role identity, that is, a conception of oneself as a man or woman in relation to the gender role requirements of one's culture.

Music and music videos can play an important part in both love-related aspects of identity formation. The portrayal of sexuality offered in popular songs can best be described as recreational. Sex is often portrayed as lighthearted fun. A recent example is Lou Bega's "Mambo Number Five." This song consists mostly of Lou describing, or at least fantasizing about, his sexual adventures with a long list of women. He describes how he desires "a little bit" of each one of them—"a little bit of Sandra in the sun/A little bit of Mary all night long," and so on. In the video, Lou sings and dances in a snazzy suit and hat, while the women who are the objects of his desire dance around him, scantily clad. They all seem to be enjoying themselves immensely. Thus, adolescents may learn from this that sex is a source of recreation, pure fun, not requiring commitment, not to be taken seriously. The sex of popular songs like "Mambo Number Five" is sex in a world without unwanted pregnancy, STDs, or even the complications of emotional relationships.

With regard to the gender role aspect of identity, songs and music videos often portray stereotyped gender roles, with males as aggressive and tough, females as vulnerable and needy or as seductresses. For example, in Limp Bizkit's recent "Nookie," the first part of the song is a hip-hop-style account of the singer's rejection by his girlfriend; this soon turns into an angry rant, as he shouts at her contemptuously, "I did it all for the nookie/The nookie/So you can take that cookie/And stick it up your (yeah!)." The male gender role, as portrayed in this song, means reacting to love-induced pain with anger.

Although analyses of songs and music videos indicate that most of them promote stereotypical gender roles, it is important not to stereotype the songs and videos themselves. They are diverse, and there are many exceptions to any generalization about them. The songs and videos of male performers like the Backstreet Boys are as emotionally vulnerable and needy as anything by female performers. As for aggressiveness, one of the most aggressive recent videos is by a female performer. In "Heartbreaker," Mariah Carey sings about her pain over her unfaithful boyfriend. In the video, Mariah and her friends trail the faithless boyfriend and his lover to a movie theater; Mariah then follows the lover to the ladies' room, where she physically assaults her! No protests were raised over the violence in this video—although it is more violent than anything that can be found in recent videos by male performers—perhaps because Mariah's violence is a violation of normative expectations for gender roles, and so is not taken seriously as promoting violence.

Coping

Another use of media common among adolescents is coping, especially in response to issues involving sexuality. Love and sex can result in frustration, disappointment, and pain, and the songs and videos popular among teens portray this side of sexuality as well. There are songs about unrequited love, songs about unfaithful lovers, songs about being lonely and wishing for a lover. All of these themes have long been staples of popular songs. Why would adolescents want to listen to songs about the unhappy side of sexual relationships? Because they know this side of sexuality all too well from their own lives, and listening to the sad songs consoles them, expresses what they have difficulty expressing themselves, and makes them feel that someone else has experienced what they are experiencing and understands how they feel.

In studies using the "beeper" method, Larson (1995) has found that adolescents spend a considerable amount of time in their rooms alone, listening to music. When they are beeped during these times, their moods are often low; they frequently report being lonely or sad. Afterward, however, they feel revived and strengthened. They use the music as a way of coping with and working through painful emotions and difficult relationship issues, often related to sexuality. Even though the music is often sad, listening to sad music in a state of sadness has the paradoxical effect of making them feel better.

Where to Now? Toward an Emic Approach

What can we conclude about music, sex, and adolescents on the basis of the research that has been conducted so far? First, we know that music is an important part of teens' daily lives, and that most of the music they listen to has sexuality as its theme. Second, we know that many of the songs and music videos most popular among teens portray gender roles in a stereotyped way, although there are notable exceptions to this rule. Third, we know that teens make use of sexually themed songs and music videos for a variety of purposes in their lives, most notably entertainment, identity formation, and coping.

These conclusions represent a solid foundation for future research on music, sex, and adolescents. Where should research be focused now, given this foundation? We would argue that more attention should be directed toward what teens themselves say about the songs and music videos that appeal to them. What we know at this point is based mostly on the judgments of scholars. It is scholars who have asserted that the songs and videos promote stereotyped gender roles. It is scholars who have made most of the judgments about the uses that teens make of songs and videos. Now we should turn our attention to what teens themselves say about why they listen to sexually themed songs and watch sexually themed videos. In anthropological terminology, we should move from an etic approach, in which outsiders make judgments about the meanings of symbols and rites and behavior in a culture, to an emic approach, in which interpretations of these meanings come from the members of the culture themselves.

Here are some of the questions that could be addressed:

- Which sexually themed songs and videos do they like most? Are there sexually themed songs and videos that they dislike or reject? If so, why?
- To what extent are they conscious of the gender stereotyping in songs and videos? Do they respond to this stereotyping positively, negatively, or with mixed feelings?
- To what extent do they believe that the portrayals of sexuality in songs and videos reflect real-life sexuality?
- Do they believe they are influenced in their sexuality by the songs and videos they listen to and watch? In what ways?

One good model of how to proceed with this line of research can be found in the work of Steele and Brown (1995). They used several methods to explore teens' views of sexuality in the media. In one method, girls were asked to record in journals whatever they witnessed in the media about "love, sex and relationships." After a month of journal keeping, each girl was interviewed about her media uses. Another method, called "autodriving," was also used, in which each teen took an interviewer on a tour of his or her bedroom, describing into a tape recorder everything in the room that held special meaning or significance. Many of these special items were media related—posters, magazine photos, concert tickets. The focus of Steele and Brown's research was on media use generally, but these and other similar methods could easily be applied specifically to the topic of sexuality and music. Through such methods, we are likely to gain new insights into the uses that teens make of sexually themed songs and music videos.

Media Messages About Youth and Race: Black Violence, White Indolence

Henry A. Giroux

In the decades of the 1980s and 1990s, Hollywood produced a host of films about the plight of young people in postmodern American culture. Henry A. Giroux examines five of these films in the article below, which is excerpted from his book *Fugitive Cultures: Race, Violence, and Youth*. The films *River's Edge* (1986), *My Own Private Idaho* (1991), *Slacker* (1991), and *Kids* (1995) all focus on white middle- and working-class teenagers. Director Ernest Dickerson's *Juice* (1992), on the other hand, depicts poor black youth in the tradition of films such as *Boys 'N the Hood* (1991), *Clockers* (1995), and *New Jersey Drive* (1995). In each of these, the overriding message about urban teenagers is that life at the end of the twentieth century delivers senseless violence, alienation, and despair. However, important differences between the representations of white and black youth tend to locate the origin of violent crime within African American communities. Young whites, it is implied, become infected by black violence like victims of an inner-city disease. The end result is what Giroux calls a "mean-

■

spirited" discourse that allows the dominant culture to deny any accountability in fostering the social conditions that encourage hopelessness, disenfranchisement, and oppression. Yet, he believes that studying popular film can be a valuable educational tool.

Henry A. Giroux is deeply interested in integrating cultural studies and education. His research encourages us to think critically about the relationships among schooling, popular culture, and decreasing opportunities for active participation in our society. He has written many articles and books in this area, including *The Mouse That Roared: Disney and the End of Innocence* (1999) and *Disturbing Pleasures: Learning Popular Culture* (1994).

YOUTH [REGULARLY] BECOME THE OBJECT OF public analysis. Headlines proliferate like dispatches from a combat zone, frequently coupling youth and violence in the interests of promoting a new kind of commonsense relationship. For example, gangsta rap artist Snoop Doggy Dogg is featured on the front cover of *Newsweek* [in 1993]. The message is that young black men are spreading violence like some kind of social disease to the mainstream public through their music. But according to *Newsweek*, the violence is not just in the music—it is also embodied in the lifestyles of the rappers who produce it. The potential victims in this case are a besieged white majority of male and female youth. Citing a wave of arrests among prominent rappers, the cover story reinforces the emergence of crime as a racially coded word for associating black youth with violence.

The statistics on youth violence point to social and economic causes of crime that lie far beyond the reach of facile stereotypes about kids today. On a national level, United States society is witnessing the effects of a culture of violence in which

> close to 12 U.S. children aged 19 and under die from gun fire each day. According to the National Center for Health Statistics, "Firearm homicide is the leading cause of death of African-American teenage boys and the second-leading cause of death of high school age children in the United States."

What is missing from news stories reported in *Newsweek* and other popular media is any critical commentary on the relationship between the spread of the culture of violence in this society and the representations of violence that saturate the mass media. In addition, there is little mention in such reports of the high numbers of infants and children killed every year through "poverty-related malnutrition and disease." Nor is the United States public informed in the popular press about "the gruesome toll of the drunk driver who is typically white." But the bad news doesn't end with a one-sided commentary on violence in the United States.

Media Oversimplifications

The representations of white youth produced by dominant media within recent years have increasingly portrayed them as lazy, sinking into a self-indulgent haze, and oblivious to the middle-class ethic of working hard and getting ahead. Of course, the dominant media do not talk about the social conditions producing a new generation of youth steeped in despair, violence, crime, poverty, and apathy. For instance, to talk about black crime without mentioning that the unemployment rate for black youth exceeds forty percent in many urban cities, serves primarily to conceal a major cause of youth unrest. Or to talk about apathy among black and white youth without analyzing the junk culture, poverty, social disenfranchisement, drugs, lack of educational opportunity, and commodification that shape daily life removes responsibility from a social system that often sees youth as simply another market niche.

With the production of goods shifting to third world countries and corporate downsizing streamlining American businesses, the present economy offers most youth the promise of service sector jobs and dim prospects for the future. Against the scarcity of opportunity, youth face a world of infinite messages and images designed to sell products or peddle senseless violence. In light of radically altered social and economic conditions, educators need to fashion alternative analyses about how youth are being constructed pedagogically, economically, and culturally within the changing nature of a postmodern culture of violence. Such a project seems vital in light of the rapidity with which market values and a commercial public culture have replaced the ethical referents for developing democratic public spheres. For example, since the 1970s, millions of jobs have been lost to capital flight, and technological change has wiped out millions more. In the last twenty years alone, the U.S. economy lost more than five million jobs in the manufacturing sector. In the face of extremely limited prospects for economic growth over the next decade, schools will be faced with an identity crisis regarding the traditional assumption that school credentials provide the best route to economic security and class mobility for a large proportion of our nation's youth. . . .

Framing Youth in Postmodern Culture

The instability and transitoriness characteristic of a diverse generation of eighteen- to twenty-five-year-olds is inextricably rooted in a larger set of postmodern cultural conditions. These conditions are informed by the following: a general loss of faith in the narratives of work and emancipation; the recognition that the indeterminacy of the future warrants confronting and living in the immediacy of experience; an acknowledgment that homelessness as a condition of randomness has replaced the security, if not misrepresentation, of home as a source of comfort and security; an experience of time and space as compressed and fragmented within a world of images that increasingly undermine the dialectic of authenticity and universalism. For many youth, plurality and contingency—whether generated by the mass media or through the dislocations spurned by the economic system, the rise of new social movements, or the crisis of representation and authority—have resulted in a world with few secure psychological, economic, or intellectual markers. This is a world in which one wanders within and between multiple borders and spaces marked by excess, otherness, and difference. This is a world in which old certainties are ruptured and meaning becomes more contingent, less indebted to the dictates of reverence and established truth. While the circumstances of youth vary across and within terrains marked by gender, racial and class differences, the modernist world of certainty and order that has traditionally policed, contained, and insulated such difference has given way. In its place is a shared postmodern space in which cultural representations merge into new hybridized forms of cultural performance, identity, and political agency. As the information highway and MTV condense time and space into what Paul Virilio [in his book *Lost Dimension*] calls "speed space," new desires, modes of association, and forms of resistance inscribe themselves into diverse spheres of popular culture. Music, rap, fashion, style, talk, politics, and cultural resistance are no longer confined to their original class and racial locations. Middle-class white kids take up the language of gangsta rap spawned in neighborhood turfs far removed from their own lives. Black youth in urban centers have created a hip hop style fashioned amid a combination of sneakers, baseball caps, and oversized clothing that integrates forms of resistance, a style later appropriated by suburban kids whose desires and identities resonate with the energy and vibrancy of rap, hip hop culture, and the new urban funk. Music displaces older forms of textuality and references a terrain of cultural production that marks the body as a site of pleasure, resistance, domination, and danger. Within this postmodern youth culture, identities merge and shift rather than becoming more uniform and static. No longer associated with any one place or location, youth increasingly inhabit shifting cultural and social spheres marked by a plurality of languages, ideologies, and cultures. Youth can no longer be seen as either bearers of counter-hegemonic cultures or as drop outs, sheepishly slacking off into an aimless and dreary accommodation to the status quo. . . .

White Youth and the Politics of Despair

For many youth, showing up for adulthood at the fin de siècle means pulling back on hope and trying to put off the future, rather than taking up the modernist challenge of trying to shape it. Popular cultural criticism has captured much of the alienation among youth and has made clear that "What used to be the pessimism of a radical fringe is now the shared assumption of a generation." Cultural studies has helped to temper this broad generalization about youth in order to investigate the more complex representations at work in the construction of a new generation of youth, representations that cannot be abstracted from the specificities of race, class, or gender. And yet, cultural studies theorists have also pointed to the increasing resistance of a twenty-something generation of youth who seem neither motivated by nostalgia for some lost conservative vision of America nor at home in the New World Order paved with the promises of the expanding electronic information highway.

While "youth" as a social construction has always been mediated, in part, as a social problem, many cultural critics believe that postmodern youth are uniquely "alien," "strange," and disconnected from the real world. For instance, in Gus Van Sant's *My Own Private Idaho* (1991), the main character, Mike, who hustles his sexual wares for money, is a dreamer lost in fractured memories of a mother who deserted him as a child. Caught between flashbacks of Mom shown in 8mm color and the video world of motley street hustlers and their clients, Mike moves through his life by falling asleep in times of stress only to awaken in different geographic locations. What holds Mike's psychic and geographic travels together is the metaphor of sleep, the dream of escape, and the ultimate realization that even memories cannot fuel hope for the future. Mike becomes a metaphor for an entire generation of lower middle-class youth forced to sell themselves in a society governed by the market, a generation that aspires to nothing, works at degrading McJobs, and lives in a world in which chance and randomness rather than struggle, community, and solidarity drive their fate.

A more disturbing picture of white, working-class youth can be found in the cult classic, *River's Edge* (1986). Teen-age anomie and drugged apathy are given painful expression in the depiction of a group of working-class youth who are casually told by their friend John that he has strangled his girlfriend, another of the group's members, and left her nude body on the riverbank. The group members at different times visit the site to view the dead body of the girl. Seemingly unable to grasp the significance of the event, the youths initially hold off from informing anyone of John's murderous act and with varying degrees of concern and self-interest try to protect the teen-age sociopath from being caught by the police. Framed in conservative terms, the youths in *River's Edge* drift through a world of broken families, blaring rock music, schooling marked by dead time, and a general indifference towards the future. In

River's Edge, history as social memory is reassembled through vignettes of 1960s types portrayed as either burned-out bikers or as the ex-radical turned teacher whose moralizing relegates politics to simple cheap opportunism. Decentered and fragmented, the youths in the movie view death, like life itself, as a mere spectacle, a matter of form rather than substance. In one sense, these youths share the quality of being "asleep" that is depicted in *My Own Private Idaho*. But what gives a more disturbing aura to *River's Edge* is that lost "innocence" gives way not merely to teen-age myopia, but also to a culture in which human life is experienced as a voyeuristic seduction, a video game, good for passing time and diverting oneself from the pervasiveness of despair. Hopelessness and indifference cancel out the language of ethical discriminations and social responsibility while elevating the immediacy of pleasure to the defining moment of agency. Exchanges among the young people in *River's Edge* appear like projections of a generation waiting either to fall asleep or to self-destruct. After talking about how he murdered his girlfriend, John blurts out "You do shit, it's done, and then you die." Another character responds, "It might be easier being dead." To which her boyfriend, a Wayne's World type, replies, "Bullshit, you couldn't get stoned anymore." In this scenario, life imitates art when committing murder and getting stoned are given equal moral weight in the formula of the Hollywood spectacle, a spectacle which in the end flattens the complex representations of youth while constructing their identities through ample servings of pleasure, violence, and indifference.

Repulsive Characters

River's Edge and *My Own Private Idaho* reveal the seamy and dark side of a youth culture while employing the Hollywood mixture of fascination and horror to titillate the audiences drawn to these films. Employing the postmodern aesthetic of revulsion, locality, randomness, and senselessness, these films present youth who appear to be constructed outside of a broader cultural and economic landscape. Hence, they become visible only through visceral expressions of psychotic behavior or the brooding experience of a self-imposed comatose alienation. *River's Edge* has spawned a number of youth films that extend and deepen its picture of youth as restless, bitter, and filled with rage. The release of *Kids* (1995) is an urban revision of the youth in *River's Edge*. The turf this time is Manhattan, and the narrative unfolds by telling the story of seventeen-year-old Telly, who describes himself as a "virgin surgeon." As the camera follows Telly and his friends through the course of a hot day in the city, an image emerges of youth who seem lost except for the thrill of sex, drugs, skateboarding, and goofing around. Casual physical brutality combines with Telly's equally brutal act of sexually transmitting the HIV virus to the girls he seduces. Utilizing an unflinching documentary style, *Kids* presents itself as a realistic look at New York youth in the 1990s. Portraying teen-agers as mindless, hormone-crazed, and indifferent to the consequences of their impulsive actions, *Kids* shatters the Disney image of innocence that all too often is invoked by conservatives when looking for role models for youth. But in *Kids*, as in a number of recent films modeled after *River's Edge*, attempts to transgress and rupture middle- and working-class depictions of youth often slip too easily into a cynicism that has as its only defense an appeal to artistic expression. *Kids* continues a long cinematic tradition of viewing youth as dull, aimless, and shorn of any idealism. As critic Jon Pareles points out, "in *Kids* . . . teen-agers [are] no longer treated as a problem to be recognized and solved but as something chronic and inevitable. . . . Numbed by drugs and mass culture, restless but affectless, they [are] portrayed [less] as alienated [than] as simply aliens."

Whereas Larry Clark, the director, invokes *Kids* as a hard-edged, representative look at urban youth, [U.S. Congressman] Newt Gingrich invokes conservative family values and *Boys Town*. Both cancel each other out. Clark evokes a paralyzing cynicism about the absence of adult authority and depravity of street life. Gingrich provides a utopian rendering of middle-class family values for white suburban youth while simultaneously offering the revamped authority of the nineteenth-century orphanage as the model for disciplining working-class, urban teen-age youth. What both positions share is an essentialist rendering of youth that is either heartful and productive or despairing and bitter. Neither position captures the complexity of representations and range of identities that youth inhabit nor the limits and possibilities that diverse youth face in the nineties. Both positions also share a racism in which black youth and the urban center become sites of contamination. For example, the white youth in *Kids* speak in a black street vernacular and appear to have appropriated the form and style of hip hop culture. The message here is that the culture of criminality is an urban culture, it is black, and it is spreading. Black teen-age welfare mothers in Gingrich's world and black street culture in Clark's universe share the same characteristics of depravity and hopelessness.

Slacker Youth

One of the more celebrated white-youth films of the 1990s is Richard Linklater's *Slacker* (1991). A decidedly low-budget film, *Slacker* attempts in both form and content to capture the sentiments of a twenty-something generation of middle-class, white youth who reject most of the values of the Reagan/Bush era in which they came of age, but have a difficult time imagining what an alternative might look like. Distinctly non-linear in its format, *Slacker* takes place in a twenty-four-hour time frame in the college town of Austin, Texas. Building upon an antinarrative structure, *Slacker* is loosely organized around brief episodes in the lives of a variety of characters, none of whom are connected to each other except to provide the pretext to lead the audience to the next character in the film. Sweeping through bookstores, coffee shops, auto-parts yards, bedrooms, and rock music clubs, *Slacker* focuses on a disparate group of young people who possess little hope in the future and drift from job to job speaking a hybrid argot of bohemian intensities and New Age pop-cult babble.

The film portrays a host of young people who randomly move from one place to the next, border crossers with little, if any, sense of where they have come from or where they are going. In this world of multiple realities, youth work in bands with names like "Ultimate Loser" and talk about being forcibly put in hospitals by their parents. One neo-punker even attempts to sell a Madonna pap smear to two acquaintances she meets in the street. "Check it out, I know it's kind of disgusting, but it's like sort of getting down to the real Madonna." This is a world in which language is wedded to an odd mix of nostalgia, pop/corn philosophy, and MTV babble. Talk is organized around comments like: "I don't know . . . I've traveled . . . and when you get back you can't tell whether it really happened to you or if you just saw it on TV." Alienation is driven inward and emerges in comments like "I feel stuck." Irony slightly overshadows a refusal to imagine the needs of anyone outside the self, forcefully precluding any kind of collective struggle. Reality seems too despairing to care about. This is humorously captured in one instance by a young man who suggests: "You know how the slogan goes, workers of the world, unite? We say workers of the world, relax." People talk but appear disconnected from themselves and each other; lives traverse each other with no sense of community or connection.

At rare moments in the film, the political paralysis of narcissistic forms of self-absorption is offset by instances in which some characters recognize the importance of the image as a vehicle for cultural production, as a representational apparatus that can not only make certain experiences available but can also be used to produce alternative realities and social practices. There is a pronounced sense in *Slacker* of youth caught in the throes of new technologies that both contain their aspirations and at the same time hold out the promise of some sense of agency. The power of the image is present in the way the camera follows characters throughout the film, at once stalking them and confining them to a gaze that is both constraining and incidental. In one scene, a young man appears in a video apartment surrounded by televisions that he claims he has had on for years. He points out that he has invented a game called a "Video Virus" in which, through the use of a special technology, he can push a button and insert himself into any screen and perform any one of a number of actions. When asked by another character what this is about, he answers: "Well, we all know the psychic powers of the televised image. But we need to capitalize on it and make it work for us instead of working for it." This theme is taken up in two other scenes. In one short clip, a graduate history student shoots the video camera he is using to film himself, indicating a self-consciousness about the power of the image and the ability to control it at the same time. In the concluding scene, a carload of people, each equipped with a Super-8 camera, drive up to a large hill and throw their cameras into a canyon. The film ends with the images being recorded by the cameras, as they cascade to the bottom of the cliff in what suggests a moment of release and liberation.

In many respects, these movies largely focus on a culture of white youth who are both terrified of and fascinated by the media, who appear overwhelmed by "the danger and wonder of future technologies, the banality of consumption, the thrill of brand names, [and] the difficulty of sex in alienated relationships." The significance of these films rests, in part, in their attempt to capture the sense of powerlessness that increasingly affects working-class and middle-class white youth. However, missing from these films as well as from the various books, articles, and reportage concerning what is often called the "Nowhere Generation," "Generation X," "13thGen," or "Slackers" is any sense of the larger political, racial, and social conditions in which youth are being framed, as well as the multiple forms of resistance and racial diversity that exist among different youth formations. What in fact should be seen as a social commentary about "dead-end capitalism" emerges simply as a celebration of refusal dressed up in a rhetoric of aesthetics, style, fashion, and solipsistic protests. Here postmodern criticism is useful but limited because of its often theoretical inability to take up the relationships between identity and power, biography and the commodification of everyday life. Such criticism also fails to address the limits of agency in an increasingly globalized world order as part of a broader project of possibility linked to issues of history, struggle, and transformation.

In spite of the totalizing image of domination that structures *River's Edge*, *My Own Private Idaho*, and *Kids*, and despite the lethal hopelessness that permeates *Slacker*, all of these films provide opportunities for examining the social and cultural contexts to which they refer in order to enlarge the range of understandings and strategies that students might bring to them to create a sense of resistance and transformation. For instance, many of my students who viewed *Slacker* did not despair over the film. They interpreted it to mean that "going slack" was a moment when young people could, with the proper resources, have time to think, move around the country, and "chill out" in order to make some important decisions about their lives. Going slack, however, might become increasingly more oppressive as the slack time became drawn out beyond their ability to end or control it. The students also pointed out that this film was made by Linklater and his friends with a great deal of energy and gusto, which in itself offers a pedagogical model for young people to take up in developing their own narratives.

Black Youth and the Violence of Race

> Unwanted as workers, underfunded as students, and undermined as citizens, minority youth seem wanted only by the criminal justice system.

While films about white youth provide a suggestive, if often politically conservative view of the twenty-something generation, they say something altogether new and problematic when placed in juxtaposition to films about black youth. With the explosion of rap music into the sphere of popular culture and with the intense debates that have emerged around the crisis of black masculinity, the issue of black nationalism, and the politics of black urban culture, it is not surprising that the black cinema should produce a series of films about the coming of age of black youth in urban America. Unlike the black exploitation films of the 1960s and 1970s, which were made by white producers for black audiences, the new wave of black cinema is being produced by black directors and aimed at black audiences. With the advent of the 1990s, Hollywood has cashed in on young, talented black directors such as Spike Lee, Allen and Albert Hughes, Charles Burnett, Ernest Dickerson, and John Singleton. Films about black youth have become big box office hits—in 1991 *New Jack City* and *Boyz N the Hood* pulled in over one hundred million dollars between them. Largely concerned with the forms of inequality, oppression, daily violence, and the diminishing hope that plague black communities in the urban war zone, the new wave of black films has attempted to accentuate the economic and social conditions that have contributed to the construction of "black masculinity and its relationship to the ghetto culture in which ideals of masculinity are nurtured and shaped."

Unlike many of the recent films about white youth, whose

coming-of-age narratives are developed within traditional sociological categories such as alienation, restlessness, and anomie, black film productions such as Ernest Dickerson's *Juice* (1992) and Nick Gomez's *New Jersey Drive* (1995), and Spike Lee's *Clockers* (1995) depict a culture of nihilism that is rooted directly in a violence whose defining principles are hopelessness, internecine warfare, cultural suicide, and social decay. It is worth noting that just as the popular press has racialized crime, drugs, and violence as a black problem, some of the most interesting films to appear recently about black youth have been given the Hollywood imprimatur of excellence and have moved successfully as crossover films to a white audience. In what follows, I want to briefly probe the treatment of black youth and the representations of masculinity and resistance in the exemplary black film, *Juice*.

Rage and Respect

Juice (street slang for respect) is the story of four Harlem African-American youth who are first portrayed as kids who engage in the usual antics of skipping school, fighting with other kids in the neighborhood, clashing with their parents about doing homework, and arguing with their siblings over using the bathroom in the morning. If this portrayal of youthful innocence is used to get a general audience to comfortably identify with these four black youths, it is soon ruptured, as the group, caught in a spiraling wave of poverty and depressed opportunities, turns to crime and violence as a way to both construct their manhood and survive their most immediate dilemmas. Determined to give their lives some sense of agency, the group moves from ripping off a record store to burglarizing a grocery market to the ruthless murders of the store owner and eventually each other. Caught in a world in which the ethics of the street are mirrored in the spectacle of TV violence, Bishop, Quincy, Raheem, and Steel (Tupac Shakur, Omar Epps, Kahalil Kain, and Jermaine Hopkins), decide, after watching James Cagney go up in a blaze of glory in *White Heat*, to take control of their lives by buying a gun and sticking up a neighborhood merchant who once chased them out of his store.

Quincy is the only black youth in the film who models a

sense of agency that is not completely caught in the confusion and despair exhibited by his three friends. Quincy is hesitant about participating in the stickup because he is a talented disc jockey and is determined to enter a local deejay contest in order to take advantage of his love of rap music and find a place for himself in the world. Positioned within the loyalty codes of the street and the protection it provides, Quincy reluctantly agrees to participate in the heist. Bad choices have major consequences in this typical big city ghetto, and Quincy's sense of hope and independence is shattered as Bishop, the most violent of the group, kills the store owner and then proceeds to murder Raheem and hunt down Quincy and Steel, since they no longer see him as a respected member of the group. Quincy eventually buys a weapon to protect himself, and in the film's final scene confronts Bishop on the roof of a run-down apartment. A struggle ensues and Bishop plunges to his death. As the film ends, one onlooker tells Quincy "You got the juice," but Quincy rejects the accolade ascribing power and prestige to him and walks away.

Juice reasserts the importance of rap music as the cultural expression of imaginable possibilities in the daily lives of black youth. Not only does rap music provide the musical score which frames the film, it also plays a pivotal role by socially contextualizing the desires, rage, and independent expression of black male artists. For Quincy, rap music offers him the opportunity to claim some "juice" among his peers while simultaneously providing him with a context to construct an affirmative identity. It also offers him the chance for real employment. Music in this context becomes a major referent for understanding how identities and bodies come together in a hip-hop culture that at its most oppositional moments is testing the limits of the American dream. But *Juice* also gestures, through the direction of Ernest Dickerson, that if violence is endemic to the black ghetto, its roots lie in a culture of violence that is daily transmitted through the medium of television. This is suggested in one powerful scene in which the group watches on television both the famed violent ending of James Cagney's *White Heat* and another scene where a news bulletin announces the death of a neighborhood friend as he attempted to rip off a local bar. In this scene, Dickerson draws a powerful relationship between what the four youth see on television and their impatience over their own lack of agency and need to take control of their lives. As Michael Dyson points out:

> Dickerson's aim is transparent: to highlight the link between violence and criminality fostered in the collective American imagination by television, the consumption of images through a medium that has replaced the Constitution and the Declaration of Independence as the unifying fiction of national citizenship and identity. It is also the daily and exclusive occupation of Bishop's listless father, a reminder that television's genealogy of influence unfolds from its dulling effects in one generation to its creation of lethal desires in the next, twin strategies of destruction when applied in the black male ghetto.

While Dyson is right in pointing to Dickerson's critique of the media, he overestimates the importance given in *Juice* to the relationship between black-on-black violence and those larger social determinants that black urban life both reflects and helps to produce. In fact, it could be argued that the violence portrayed in *Juice* and similar films such as *Boyz N the Hood*, *New Jack City*, *Sugar Hill*, *Menace II Society*, *Jason's Lyric*, and *Clockers* "feeds the racist national obsession that black men and their community are the central locus of the American scene of violence."

Limiting the Focus

Although the violence in these films is traumatizing in an effort to promote an antiviolence message, it is also a violence that is hermetically sealed within the walls of the black urban ghetto. While the counterpart of this type of violence in controversial white films such as *Reservoir Dogs* is taken up by most critics as part of an avant-garde aesthetic, the documentary-style violence in the recent wave of black youth films often reinforces for middle-class viewers the assumption that such violence is endemic to the black community. The only salvation gained in portraying such inner-city hopelessness is that it be noticed so that it can be stopped from spreading like a disease into the adjoining suburbs and business zones that form a colonizing ring around black ghettoes. Because films such as *Juice* do not self-consciously rupture dominant stereotypical as-sumptions that make race and crime synonymous, they often suggest a kind of nihilism that Cornel West describes as "the lived experience of coping with a life of horrifying meaning-lessness, hopelessness and (most important) lovelessness."

Unfortunately, West's notion of nihilism is too tightly drawn around black communities. While it may claim to pay sufficient attention to the loss of hope and meaning among black youth, it fails to connect the specificity of black nihilism to the alienation that results from systemic inequality, calcu-lated injustice, and moral indifference that operate as a daily regime of brutality and oppression for so many working-class and black youth in this country. Itabari Njeri forcefully cap-tures the failure of such an analysis and the problems that films such as *Juice* and *Clockers*, in spite of the best intentions of their directors, often reproduce. Commenting on another coming-of-age black youth film, *Menace II Society*, she writes:

> The nation cannot allow nearly 50% of black men to be un-employed, as is the case in many African-American commu-nities. It cannot let schools systematically brand normal black children as uneducable for racist reasons, or permit the continued brutalization of blacks by police, or have black adults take out their socially engendered frustrations on each other and their children and not yield despair and dysfunction. This kind of despair is the source of the ni-hilism Cornel West described. Unfortunately, the black male-as-menace film genre often fails to artfully tie this ni-hilism to its poisonous roots in America's system of inequal-ity. And because it fails to do so, the effects of these toxic forces are seen as causes.

In both pedagogical and political terms, the reigning films about black youth that have appeared since 1990 may have gone too far in producing narratives that employ the commercial strategy of reproducing graphic violence and then moralizing about its effects. Violence in these films is tied to a self-destructiveness and senselessness that shocks but often fails to inform audiences about either its wider determinations or the audience's possible complicity with such violence. The effects of such films tend to reinforce for white, middle-class America the comforting belief that violence as both a state of mind and a site of social relations is always somewhere else—in that strangely homogenized social formation known as "black" youth.

It is important to note that films such as *Juice* and more recently *Clockers* refrain from romanticizing violence; in the concluding scenes of *Juice*, Quincy does not want the juice if it means leading a life in which violence is the only capital that has any exchange value in African-American communities. Similarly, Strike, the teen-age crack dealer in *Clockers*, neither glamorizes nor embodies the fascination with violence so often found in black youth films. The violence Strike sees all around him and increasingly experiences himself is played out in not only the revolt of his conscience, but also in a bleeding ulcer that debilitates his body. If there is a refusal to endorse the spectacle of violence in films such as *Juice* and *Clockers*, it is undercut by the riveting assumption that there are no positive choices, no way out, for black men in these communities. The violence of the streets is matched by the violence of confinement and the loss of any notion of racial justice or social agency. As violence becomes hermetic in these films, any notion of resistance, social change, and collective agency disappears as well.

The Value of Viewing

One pedagogical challenge presented by *Juice* is for educators and students to theorize about why Hollywood is investing in films about black youth that overlook the complex representations that structure African-American communities. Such an inquiry can be taken up by looking at the work of black feminist filmmakers such as Julie Dash, who offers black women powerful and complex representations in *Daughters of the Dust*, or the work of Leslie Harris, whose film *Just Another Girl on the IRT* challenges the misogyny that structures the films currently available about black male youth. Another challenge for educators involves trying to understand why black, urban, male youth readily identify with the wider social representations of sexism, homophobia, and misogyny, in exchange for a form of "respect" that comes at such a high cost to themselves and the communities in which they live. It is important to engage films about black youth in order to both understand the pedagogies that silently structure their representations and how such representations pedagogically work to educate both black and white audiences. Needless to say, these films should not be dismissed because they are in their worst moments reductionistic, sexist, or one-dimensional in their portrayal of the rite of passage of black male youth. At most, they become a marker for understanding how complex representations of black youth get lost in racially coded films that point to serious problems in the urban centers, but do so in ways that erase the accountability of the dominant culture and racist institutions, on the one hand, and any sense of viable hope, possibility, resistance, and struggle on the other. Furthermore, educators and other cultural workers must address the critical importance of representations of blackness emerging from black artists, while taking into account that such lived experience might not translate into a progressive understanding of the social relations depicted.

Contemporary films about black youth offer a glimpse into the specificity of otherness; that is, they cross a cultural and racial border and in doing so perform a theoretical service in making visible what is often left out of the dominant politics of representation. And it is in the light of such an opening that the possibility exists for educators and other cultural workers to take up the relationship among culture, power, and identity in ways that grapple with the complexity of youth and the intersection of race, class, and gender formations.

EXAMINING POP CULTURE

Representing Teenagers in Pop Culture

Popular Music Reflects Teens' Attitudes About School

B. Lee Cooper

What can we learn from the lyrics of teenager hit tunes? B. Lee Cooper argues that they provide insight into the preoccupations, values, and priorities of young people. His extensive study discussed in this essay highlights a central theme in music from the rock era: School is a primary source of frustration for students. While occasional admiration for exceptional teachers is not absent, a critical attitude pervades most songs about school life between 1955 and 1980. Lyrics depict ignorant and insensitive instructors, prison-like schools, and irrelevant curricula. Cooper entreats us to heed the persistent message and acknowledge a need for reevaluation and revision of formal education.

Educated as a historian, Cooper currently serves as vice president for academic affairs/dean of the college at Reinhardt College, Waleska, Georgia. He has written numerous books and articles about contemporary music and the value of popular culture as an educational tool. One of many notable contributions is his three-volume work *Rock Music in American Popular Culture* (1994–1999).

■

FORMAL EDUCATION CONSTITUTES A KEY FOE for angry rap chanters and aggressive heavy metal head-bangers. Their words depicting school experiences are invariably harsh. But '90s lyrical indictments of teachers, principals, and curricula as unresponsive, unintelligible, and irrelevant can be traced to the earliest rock performers. In fact, throughout the first quarter century of the post–Big Band Era (1955–1980), audio portrayals of junior and senior high school experiences ranged from mockery to rage. With ancestral roots as deep as Chuck Berry and images as vitriolic as those vocalized by Pink Floyd, it is little wonder that present-day singers and songwriters continue to deride public schooling. The following commentary provides a detailed analysis of recordings from the early Rock Era that illustrate adolescent disenchantment with institutionalized learning.

Despite the cacophony of criticisms from many reform-minded pressure groups, observations from one key group—students, the subject of the whole educational enterprise—are generally ignored. But youth has not remained mute. Scholars simply have not applied their critical skills to a wide enough variety of resources on this issue. Popular music, a principal artifact of youth culture, gives voice to a broad range of concerns, values, and priorities of young people. A thorough analysis of scores of popular songs demonstrates that lyrics consistently depict formal schooling as dehumanizing, irrelevant, alienating, laughable, isolating, and totally unworthy of any link with the Socratic tradition. Some might argue, of course, that popular music does not actually reflect the perceptions of the audience per se. Most hit tunes, after all, are not written by students. Pop recordings are simply products of market devices. But lyricists and singers are clearly the troubadours of contemporary young people. To claim that they do not represent student perceptions because they are no longer students themselves is equivalent to arguing that balladeers of medieval Europe did not reflect the culture of courtly society because they were not part of the aristocracy. Troubadours in any age are honored precisely *because* their musical messages resound with the values and imagination of their audience. Indeed, modern troubadours are probably better mirrors of the culture in whose name they sing than their feudal predecessors. Unlike minstrels of old, modern rock musicians, although no longer students when they write or perform their music, have actually been in the classroom. Their medieval counterparts were never aristocrats.

Popular music has not always portrayed schooling in a negative way. Education appeared less frequently as a theme in the pre–Rock Era, but, when it did, lyrics were usually nostalgic, as in "School Days" or "In the Little Red School House." In addition, earlier education themes were generally oriented toward college students, even though only a small proportion of young people attended universities prior to 1950. From the 1906 recording of "College Life," through "Collegiate," "The Varsity Drag," "Betty Co-Ed," "The Sweetheart of Sigma Chi," to "The Whiffenpoof Song" in 1936, early popular music dealing with education emphasized the carefree joys of campus social life. Ironically, in an age when university attendance has become the norm, very few rock songs deal with college life. Most focus exclusively on public school experiences, particularly on secondary schooling. And, with very few exceptions—the Arbors' "Graduation Day" and the Beach Boys' "Be True to Your School"—the sentiments communicated are anything but nostalgic.

Images of Schools

> "School days, school days,
> Dear old golden rule days,
> Readin' and writin' and 'rithmatic,
> Taught to the tune of a hickory stick."

Sentiments of good times, firm discipline, and inculcation of basic communication and computation skills featured in the traditional tune "School Days" represent learning perceptions from another era. Whether accurate or inaccurate, realistic or idealistic, this song came to symbolize formal education during the early twentieth century. But, as Bob Dylan noted during the '60s, "the times they are a-changin.'" In 1954, the U.S. Supreme Court ordered American education to cease the practice of utilizing racially segregated, "separate but equal" learning arenas. But the integration of public schools wasn't the only revolution occurring in mid-'50s America. Currents of popular music were also beginning to flow more swiftly. The rock 'n' roll floodtide emerged when country music tunes and rhythm and blues songs found synthesizing spokesmen in Bill Haley, Otis Williams, Elvis Presley, Chuck Berry, Carl Perkins, and Jerry Lee Lewis. This popular music rampage, aided by influential disc jockeys, several technological recording inventions, motion picture hype (*Blackboard Jungle*), and improved record company promotional techniques, launched a fundamental change in America's musical tastes as well as in lyrical imagery. . . .

No systematic, comprehensive statement of public school criticism can be found in the grooves of popular recordings. Nevertheless, several key ideas are present. Between 1955 and 1980, previously dominant preachment and pretense images of schooling were directly challenged. Lyrical idealism was not totally absent, of course. Admiration for teachers who were bright, deeply committed to learning, concerned about pupils, and engaged in a constant battle to overcome ignorance was eulogized in tunes like "To Sir With Love" and "Welcome Back." But a much more critical tone dominates the majority of lyrical commentaries about schooling. Teachers are generally condemned for being ignorant of student feelings ("Bird Dog"), for pursuing irrelevant classroom topics ("Wonderful World"), for corrupting student idealism ("The Logical Song"), and for intentionally stifling the development of pupils' social and political awareness ("Another Brick in the Wall"). It is difficult to imagine a more blatant denunciation of the entire educational system than Paul Simon's introductory phrases in "Kodachrome," where he dismisses his high school learning as "crap," marvels that he can still think, and ends with an ungrammatical claim that his ignorance doesn't prevent him from seeing "writing on the wall.". . .

The classroom is generally depicted as the dictatorial domain of a teaching tyrant who doesn't realize how mean her looks are, as Chuck Berry snorts in "School Days." Activities which occur in classrooms are conducted in lock-step, intimidating, teacher-directed fashion. A student like the Coasters' "Charlie Brown" may walk into the classroom cool and slow, but then he'd better become quiet, orderly, and without guile. By contrast, the hallways are always alive with noise. Rigidly enforced classroom silence and cerebral irrelevance give way to cacophonous peer chatter and delirious social interaction. Discussions of cars, sex, smokes, food, films, and immediate wants and needs occur in the jostling, locker-slamming hallway atmosphere. School corridors also lead to freedom (". . . down the hall and into the street" ["School Days"]); to a secret cigarette break in the restroom ("Smokin' in the Boys Room"); to a luncheon record hop ("High School Dance"); to more private activities in outdoor recreation areas ("Me and Julio Down in the Schoolyard"); and to the parking lot filled with decorated cars and vans. The key word to describe most lyrical observations about the school building is—escape. Even those songs which laud memories of bygone secondary school experiences, such as Adrian Kimberly's "Pomp and Circumstance," praise commencement as the eternal relief felt by all alumni. This escapist theme is also clearly delineated in songs that depict the annual freedom period from June through August: Gary U.S. Bonds' "School Is Out," the Jamies' "Summertime, Summertime," and Alice Cooper's "School's Out."

Images of Students

Lyrical images of students vary greatly. Clear recognition of peer pressures and special interest groups within each school is illustrated in the Beach Boys' "I Get Around," Dobie Gray's "In Crowd," and Connie Frances' "Where the Boys Are." The isolation of nonconforming individuals and out-groups is depicted in The Crystals' "He's a Rebel," The Shangri-Las' "Leader of the Pack," Carol Jarvis' "Rebel," and Janis Ian's "At Seventeen" and "Society's Child." Although they comprise the most heterogeneous group within the public educational system, students are lyrically characterized as the least franchised ("Summertime Blues"), most harassed ("Yackety Yak"), most regimented ("Another Brick in the Wall"), least trusted ("Smokin' in the Boy's Room"), most humorous ("Charlie Brown" and "My Boy Flat Top"), most victimized ("My Generation" and "Society's Child"), and least understood ("It Hurts to Be Sixteen" and "You and Me Against the World").

Students are usually described as physically active and singularly noncontemplative. In fact, as Sam Cooke declared in his 1960 hit "Wonderful World," the typical romantic high school youth boasts (in parallel double negatives) about his ignorance of history, biology, a science book, and French. Nearly two decades later, Art Garfunkel, Paul Simon, and James Taylor revived Cooke's "(What a) Wonderful World" with yet another anti-intellectual refrain, adding the Middle Ages, the Rise and Fall, and "nothin' at all" to the areas of ignorance.

This sense of educational futility is a dominant element in popular lyrics. Paul Simon's 1973 song "Kodachrome," which begins with a stunning indictment of academic irrelevance, was followed three years later by an even more negative analysis of post–high school life in "Still Crazy After All These Years." This self-assessment was shared with a former high school girlfriend. Several other songs also capture poignant vignettes of post–high school reflections. Tunes like Bob Seger's "2 + 2 = ?" explore the meaning of a school friend's senseless death in Vietnam; Alice Cooper's "Eighteen" examines the "I'm a boy, but I'm a man" predicament of a recent high school graduate; and Bob Dylan's "Subterranean Homesick Blues" presents an image of an illogical, mean-spirited society which awaits formally educated, but non-streetwise youngsters.

Images of Teachers and Principals

Adults who control the environment within public schools are neither admired nor respected. Even those few songs which praise individual teachers—"Mr Lee" by The Bobbettes, "To Sir With Love" by Lulu, and "Abigail Beecher" by Freddy Cannon—offer sharp, derogatory contrasts between the caring behavior and independent actions of their favored instructors and the general demeanor of the majority of teachers who are boobs, bumpkins, and boors. Chuck Berry, the Coasters, The Who, Janis Ian, Paul Simon, and dozens of other singers reinforce the simple message chanted by Pink Floyd in his ungrammatical warning to teachers to "leave them kids alone!"

If teachers are fools, antiquarians, babysitters, arbitrary actors, and persons generally out of touch with reality, principals are outright villains with malevolent motives and totalitarian instincts. Although very few lyrical commentaries are addressed directly to the chief administrative officers in schools, the implications of managerial rule-making authority and the harsh methods of discipline enforcement abound. The jangling bell system, a lock-step, class-to-class routine, deperson-alized hall passes, regimented class changes, overly brief lunch periods ("School Days"), and dozens of other system-defining annoyances are passively attributed to the principal, though they are actively enforced by teachers.

Most distressing is the fact that teachers are universally de-fined antithetically to their students. They are without com-mon sense ("Bird Dog"), cynical ("The Logical Song"), hu-morless ("School Days" and "Charlie Brown"), out of touch with personal problems, and representative of a system of thought and action that hides from, rather than confronts, genuine social problems ("Another Brick in the Wall"). Even John Sebastian's laudatory "Welcome Back"—a tribute to a single teacher's devotion and responsibility—carefully notes the exception to the norm. . . .

Image of Education

"Please tell me who I am?" This question paraphrases the more positively stated dictum, "Know Thyself" inscribed on the Temple of Delphi. But the question is central to the lyrical crit-icism of formal education posed by Supertramp in their 1979 hit "The Logical Song." Echoing Rousseau's naturalistic edu-cational premise, the lyric depicts an untutored youngster who views life as wonderful, beautiful, and magical. Then, he is sent away to school where he learns to be clinical, logical, cynical, sensible, responsible, and practical. Pink Floyd's "Another Brick in the Wall" challenged the formal educational system with a more direct stinging, chanting attack on education itself, thought control, dark sarcasm in classes, and teacher interfer-ence with students. The Supertramp/Pink Floyd assertions seem far more deep-rooted and radical than the humorous, ex-asperated tales of Chuck Berry and the Coasters. Yet they are logical extensions of lyrical critiques presented by Janis Ian, Paul Simon, and others who are understandably appalled by the failure of American education to meet or even to approach in practice its oft-repeated ideals. The laudable goals of foster-ing human dignity, creativity, freedom, individualism, knowl-edge, diversity, and objectivity are submerged in public schools beneath a miasma of regimentation, indoctrination, cynicism, arbitrariness, authoritarianism, local morality, and cultural bias.

The disembodied voice of American youth—popular recordings—chant a consistent, sad refrain.

It might be easy to argue, in defense of enlightened teaching, that few popular songs could appropriately detail the virtues of an inspired history lecture, the potential delight of analyzing Shakespeare's sonnets, or the feeling of confidence gained by conducting a successful chemistry experiment. However, the weight of contemporary lyrical evidence is conclusive. Good teaching is an exception; inept classroom performance is expected and received. Similarly, belittling ridicule rather than reinforcing praise is the norm for dealing with students—from principals, from parents, from instructors, and (not infrequently) from insensitive, conforming peers as well. The public school arena is a polity that Aristotle would probably label an "unjust society"—where the "just" person (logical, creative, sensitive, democratic) will either become or be perceived as alienated and rebellious. What is even more regrettable, though, is the apparent success of this system in sustaining itself.

Where Do Students Learn?

If public schools are such ineffective sources of learning, then how do young people gain knowledge? Although tunesmiths provide a spectacular variety of options, they seem to concur on one point. Most valuable ideas, information, social contacts, feelings, beliefs, and personal values are secured through individual experience outside of the classroom. Recorded commentaries argue "I Gotta Be Me," "My Way," "Just the Way You Are," and "You May Be Right." The individualistic road through life is not necessarily solipsistic, nor alienating, nor narcissistic. Once again, lyrical images of community pressures ("Town Without Pity"), peer criticisms ("Sticks and Stones"), parental restraints ("Yackety Yak" and "Summertime Blues"), church irrelevance ("Only the Good Die Young"), political skullduggery ("Won't Get Fooled Again"), and wage labor meaninglessness ("Wake Me, Shake Me," "Get a Job," "Take This Job and Shove It," and "Workin' at the Carwash Blues") tend to hinder personal development through outside-of-school contacts.

This study does not intend to suggest that 1955–1980 recordings are devoid of paeans to the joy of intellectual growth and self discovery. Abundant examples illustrate constructive personal experiences. Some are humorous, such as "Spiders and Snakes," "Mr. Businessman," and "Dead End Street;" some are serious, such as "Question," "Who Will Answer," and "Eve of Destruction;" and some are poignant, such as "Color Him Father," "Son of Hickory Holler's Tramp," and "Patches." In each of these instances, of course, the learning is directly connected to individual perceptions of personally meaningful life events. No organized, administered, routinized system can replace authentic human experience. Rousseau may not be correct about a person's natural bent toward goodness; however, Thoreau's concept of simplifying in order to enrich each man's life might serve as a guiding principle to revise and reshape formal education. Real learning, if those messages communicated in popular songs are to be believed, is intrinsically personal. Therefore, the bureaucratic public educational system of the United States is antithetical to the process of individual growth. Is it any wonder that school consolidation, classroom and curriculum regimentation, computerization, teacher unionization, and other facets of mass education have further alienated so many students? Images of schools as minimal security detention centers ("Smokin' in the Boy's Room," "School Days," and "Charlie Brown") are more depressing than comic. The hard work of good principals, creative and caring teachers, and concerned parents to improve community schools may be futile because their efforts fail to take into account several fundamental educational prerequisites. Learning is intrinsically personal. The needs and experiences of American students defy the factory-like organizational patterns which may have worked well during the post–World War I period. The shifting technology of American society—a car culture, a television culture, a computer culture—is dramatically altering the lives of young and old alike. Similarly, events of the past forty years, ranging from the launching of Sputnik and the prolonged Vietnam conflict to the attempted assassination of Ronald Reagan and the rise of Japanese economic dominance, have altered the collective psyche of students. But the primary audio barometer of America's youth culture—popular music—continues to illustrate the expectations, observations, assumptions, and goals of school-age people.

The First Realistic Portrayals of Juvenile Delinquency in Film

Laurence Miller

Juvenile delinquency cases in the United States multiplied after World War II. In spite of growing public interest and alarm, the motion picture industry tended to avoid the subject. Even the genre of film noir (1940–1959), with its emphasis on danger and corruption, largely ignored depicting the criminal life of young people. Yet Laurence Miller argues that the few film noir depictions of juvenile delinquency are worth attention because they were the first to attempt a realistic representation of delinquent subcultures. These early films paved the way for the more famous juvenile delinquency films of the 1950s, such as *The Wild One* (1953), *The Blackboard Jungle* (1955), and *Rebel Without a Cause* (1955). In the article below, Miller discusses this "golden age" of delinquency films and analyzes the influential contributions of its film noir predecessors.

Much of Laurence Miller's writing and research combines his interests in psychology and film. He is currently a professor of psychology at Western Washington University.

∎

Laurence Miller, "Juvenile Delinquency in Films During the Era of Film Noir: 1940–1959," *Images of Youth: Popular Culture as Educational Ideology*, edited by Michael A. Oliker and Walter P. Krolikowski. New York: Peter Lang, 2001. Copyright © 2001 by Peter Lang Publishing, Inc. Reproduced by permission.

A FEW YEARS AFTER THE END OF WORLD WAR II, there was a sharp increase in juvenile arrest rates and cases heard in court (Lunden, 1964). This increase was paralleled by increased public attention and scrutiny. A vigilant, aroused, fearful, worried, and concerned public composed of the various media, parents, educators, social service agencies, and government and law enforcement officials intently discussed and argued the issues.

Interestingly, the motion picture industry did not markedly exploit this awareness and concern over juvenile delinquency. Given the number of films released during and after the war, extremely few dealt with the subject. A number of possible explanations can be posited. Perhaps the film industry believed that the public would not be receptive to such films, given the fear and anxiety that juvenile delinquency seemed to elicit in people. Afraid of running afoul of the Motion Picture Producers and Distributors of America (MPPDA) Film Code, the industry promised to commit itself to wholesome entertainment and not to demean correct standards of living. Transgressions in accepted morality in areas of crime, sex, and vulgarity—which juvenile delinquency could be expected to touch on—were to be avoided. . . .

It was only through film noir that any kind of realistic portrayal of juvenile delinquency and its vagaries was presented during the '40s. But, even though juvenile delinquency is a natural subject matter for film noir, very few films that can be called film noir dealt with it. In the two decades of film noir, from 1940 through 1959, which encompassed more than five hundred films, only four dealt with juvenile delinquency, and the first films did not appear until 1949. For those unfamiliar with film noir, a few words about it are in order.

The Genre of Film Noir

Film noir is one of the most extensively studied and influential film genres. Film noir ("dark" or "black") is a French term which identifies a body of American films perceived by European film scholars as having cohesive and consistent themes. Film noir contrasts markedly with other film genres produced at the same time. Film noir viewed the world as an implacable, harsh, and dangerous place devoid of hope. Fate rules one's life.

Film noir had a "black" mood as it presented a sinister nether-world of immorality, evil, violence, corruption, betrayal, venge-ance, doom, criminal behavior, obsession, psychopathology, alienation, and human frailty. Film noir provided an uncom-promising and unsentimental portrayal of human behavior and the environment. These noir themes were complemented by flashbacks, voice-overs, and, especially, by a unique visual style which stressed black and white photography, location shooting (often at night), odd camera angles and shadows, and rain-slicked streets. . . .

Four juvenile delinquency films noirs were made. All four are realistic and powerful portrayals of juvenile delinquency in America during the '40s that accurately reflect the prevailing sociological theories of the time. And all four are totally re-moved from the slapstick silliness of the Bowery Boys films. Three of the four films were released during the middle of the film noir cycle in 1949. The fourth was released at the very end of the noir cycle in 1959.

They Live by Night

Two of the four films were directed by Nicholas Ray: *They Live by Night* and *Knock on Any Door*. Both were released in 1949. *They Live by Night* was based on the novel *Thieves Like Us* by Edward Anderson. In an early draft in 1946 Ray set the tone of the film when he wrote that it was a tender and tragic love story rather than a brutal crime movie. It was a morality story about two ill-starred, lost kids, much in the vein of *Romeo and Juliet*. This observation tellingly and clearly reveals Ray's em-phasis on emotionality and intimacy in his storytelling and his sympathy for his juvenile protagonists, tragically enmeshed in a cruel and unforgiving world. . . .

They Live by Night opens with a warm and affectionate shot of the two lovers, Farley Granger as Bowie and Cathy O'Don-nell as Keechie. This happiness is frozen in subtitles written across the screen warning that Bowie and Keechie were never adequately prepared for life in this world. The lovers look up, startled, the credits appear, and we know they are doomed. Two hardened criminals, Chickimaw and T-Dub, engineer a prison break and take Bowie with them. Bowie, now 23, has been serv-ing a life sentence for murder since age 16. The film tells the story of Bowie and his girlfriend Keechie and their doomed struggle to break away from the past and a life of crime and lead a normal existence. However, Bowie is sucked back into crime, ultimately betrayed, and killed by the police. . . .

Knock on Any Door

Knock on Any Door was Ray's second film, although it was released nine months prior to *They Live by Night*, which was completed in 1947. The film was adapted from Willard Motley's novel. . . . Much of the film plays like a didactic sociological tract, espousing older prewar theories of delinquency that were now being supplemented by newer and different theories. The film is consistent with the theories of Clifford Shaw and Henry McKay. In the late '20s and '30s, they stated that delinquency reflected a geographical pattern. It proliferated in areas of high crime, social and urban disorganization, and a large immigrant population. Also, delinquency was not differentiated from other types of criminal behavior but was one stage in the developmental cycle of a criminal progressing toward increasingly serious crimes. . . .

Knock on Any Door tells the story of Nick Romano (John Derek), a juvenile delinquent with a record of petty crime, who is tried for the murder of a policeman killed during a robbery. Via flashbacks, the causes for Romano's criminal behavior are explored: poverty, no father, the oppression and vicissitudes of slum life. Nick's attempts to reform fail; his desperate and pregnant wife commits suicide; and, blinded with grief and rage, Nick commits robbery and murder. His lawyer makes a passionate speech to the jury, emphasizing how Nick's environment, immigrant background, reform school, and an indifferent society shaped Nick from a potentially good person into the criminal he became. Nevertheless, Nick is found guilty and sentenced to die. With an air of resignation, the lawyer observes that we all share Nick's guilt, that he could have risen rather than fallen, and that we can find him behind any door.

City Across the River

City Across the River was also released in 1949. . . . The film covers some of the same territory as *Knock on Any Door* but also anticipates some of the themes of the juvenile delinquency films of the '50s. The film opens with an introductory state-ment by newspaper columnist Drew Pearson:

> The city where juvenile crime flourishes always seems to be the City Across the River [Brooklyn, which is across the East River from Manhattan]. But don't kid yourself—it could be your city, your state, your house. It could just as well happen in any other large city where slum conditions undermine personal security and take their toll in juvenile delinquency.

The film tells the story of Frankie Cusack, who, according to Pearson, is "going down a confused road toward gangsterdom, toward murder." Frankie lives in a Brooklyn tenement. Both of his parents work, and Frankie spends his unsupervised free time with a gang of juvenile delinquents, the Dukes. At first re-luctant to involve himself in the gang's criminal activities, he eventually becomes incorporated into the gang as a result of peer pressure and rebellion against his poor living conditions. His parents, concerned at Frankie's drift, try to buy a house in a suburb well away from Brooklyn, but his mother becomes sick, and the house money has to be used to pay medical bills. Frankie eventually becomes involved in the accidental shooting of a teacher and a friend and is apprehended by the police. . . .

[City Across the River] was the first juvenile delinquency film to deal with organized gangs, which emerged fully into public consciousness and became staple fare for films in the '50s. Drew Pearson's allusion to juvenile delinquency as oc-curring anywhere also anticipated '50s themes, which took delinquency into middle-class suburbs (although, in the same sentence, Pearson harks back to delinquency as being a prod-uct of the urban slums). The film reflected newer theories that viewed juvenile delinquency as a product of family disorgani-zation. Both of Frankie's parents worked and so were not available much of the time to provide guidance and act as role models. . . .

The New Juvenile Delinquency

The '50s marked an important transition in the treatment of juvenile delinquency, by society, sociological theory, and films. In a sense, the '50s marked what can be called a Golden Age of juvenile delinquency, in terms of significant increases in its frequency, emergence of new types, and the concern and attention paid to it by the public and the various media. Beginning in 1948, the incidence of juvenile delinquency rose significantly faster than the increase of juveniles in the population. The number of cases more than doubled, while the number of juveniles increased by only about 20 percent. . . .

The '50s also ushered in a "new" juvenile delinquency. This new delinquency was a product of the rapid and profound changes in all levels of society which occurred during World War II and the postwar years: technological and cultural changes; demographic shifts in population; pressure on the family; urbanization and suburbanization; changing populations in schools; increased affluence; the rise of mass media, especially television; increased mobility; and relaxation of older moral standards. In society, these changes were correlated with new forms of delinquency, and old forms became much more common and vicious: auto theft, gang rumbles, drugs and alcoholism, matricide and patricide, sexual offenses, vandalism, etc. Additionally, delinquency moved visibly beyond the borders of urban slums into suburbia and the middle classes. All of these changes occurred in the context of an emerging youth culture which viewed itself as separate and distinct from—and often hostile and opposed to—adult society. With its own music, dress, interests, outlook on life, and code of conduct, a populous and influential constituency had emerged. Juvenile delinquency was viewed as a subculture within the larger youth culture.

The motion picture industry was certainly aware of these changing trends in delinquency and of the public's concern. A potentially vast audience of concerned adults and youths existed for these films. The era and social climate were right for the release of films which dealt with this new delinquency. There were three films which best captured the themes of the new delinquency during the '50s: *The Wild One* (1953), *The Blackboard Jungle* (1955), and *Rebel Without a Cause* (1955). . . .

Moving Away from Noir: *The Wild One*

The first of the key films, *The Wild One*, was released in 1953. It was produced by Stanley Kramer, directed by Laslo Benedek, and written by John Paxton. The film deals with the effects and repercussions of the invasion and occupation of a small California town by two motorcycle gangs. The film was based on an actual incident in which a biker gang took over Hollister, California, in 1947 and destroyed it.

The gangs are led by Johnny (Marlon Brando) and Chino (Lee Marvin). Like the characters in *They Live by Night*, the individuals in *The Wild One* are not teenagers but young adults in their twenties and thirties. However, the film is included in this essay because it dealt with a form of the new delinquency, biker gangs, and, most importantly, because the film introduced themes that were central to later juvenile delinquency films of the '50s. The primary theme of *The Wild One* is the conflict and antagonism between the bikers and society, as represented by the decent townspeople and police. The contempt each has for the others' values is apparent from the bikers' willful disruption of the town, their utter disrespect for its citizens, and the disparaging observations each makes about the other. . . .

Yet, it is apparent that, consciously or unconsciously, the sympathies of the film lay with the bikers. This is most obvious in casting Marlon Brando in the lead role. Brando's brilliant, compelling, and charismatic performance provided a model of the alienated hero of the '50s. (The famous poster of Brando sitting on his bike hung on the walls of many a youth, this author included.) On the one hand, he is "bad"—but bad in a seductive and alluring way: a born leader; tough and sullen, but also sensitive and vulnerable; an accomplished street fighter; irresistible to women; a young man who goes his own way and defies an uncomprehending and stuffy society. Brando's portrayal became an icon of the alienated and disaffected youth culture and paved the way for the other two key films of the '50s, *The Blackboard Jungle* and *Rebel Without a Cause*. . . .

Young Versus Old: *The Blackboard Jungle*

The Blackboard Jungle was released in 1955. It was written and directed by Richard Brooks and based on the novel by Evan Hunter. In a few respects, the film harks back to the juvenile delinquency films of the earlier era. It takes place in a lower-class urban technical-trade all-male high school. It reflected older sociological theories that focused on the breakdown of the home caused by the war. A policeman intones that they were children during World War II. Their fathers were in the army and their mothers worked. They had no life at home or in the church or any place they could go. So they formed gangs, and gang leaders became their parents.

However, the film is right on the mark in expressing, like *The Wild One*, the clash between the emerging youth culture and adults, as seen in the ongoing conflict between the teachers and administration and the students who do not want to be there. The film accomplishes this more pointedly and convincingly than does *The Wild One*. By taking place in an urban environment, the characters and situations can be more easily identified with. The music reflects the youth culture's music. The credits unfold to Bill Haley and the Comets' *Rock Around the Clock*, a rock and roll anthem. The song's call to "rock around the clock tonight" obviously promotes an ethic of pleasure counter to the Puritan work ethic of adult society. . . .

The film, like *The Wild One*, has the obligatory warning at the beginning on public concern about the causes and effects of juvenile delinquency, especially as it affects schools, and the need for public awareness as the preamble to solving the problem. And an upbeat ending: The two hard case and incorrigible delinquents are subjugated and expelled and the other students are won over and become productive and hardworking students.

However, the lure and seductiveness of the defiance and opposition to the adult culture by the delinquents was unmistakable and irresistible (a situation not at all unlike that of white culture's attraction to the ominous themes of violence and misogyny of rap music). Youths in the audience repeatedly danced in the aisles and cheered the defiance, violence, and terror inflicted by the students on the administration and teachers. The film was a box office success and aroused significant and widespread opposition and alarm among adults. . . .

Breaking New Ground: *Rebel Without a Cause*

The most famous and influential juvenile delinquency film of the '50s, *Rebel Without a Cause*, was released shortly after *The Blackboard Jungle*. The title came from a book written by Robert

Lindner in 1944, a study of imprisoned psychopaths. . . .

Rebel Without a Cause broke new ground in the treatment of juvenile delinquency. It was the first study of delinquency in middle-class suburbs rather than urban slums. This reflects the emergence of middle-class delinquency in the '50s, as a manifestation of the "new" delinquency. It is emphasized in the film by the conflicts between the middle-class youths, dressed in sport coat and tie or dresses, and the more traditional hoodlum types from the other side of the tracks, who dress in jeans, T-shirts, and black leather jackets.

The sympathies of the film lay wholly with its three protagonists, played by James Dean, Sal Mineo, and Natalie Wood. The sources of their problems and delinquent behavior reside in the dysfunctional family relationship each has and in their search for an emotionally fulfilling, warm, and secure family life. Dean's meek father is dominated by his mother, who is also highly critical of Dean. Wood seeks the love of her father and has to contend with a jealous mother. Mineo lives with his divorced mother and is ignored by her and by his absent father. In a touching scene in an abandoned house, the three attempt to form a family, an attempt that is short-lived and ends in tragedy. It is the despair and unhappiness with their family life that leads the three youths to search for fulfillment outside their families and in delinquency. This alienation is reinforced by two key scenes in the Griffith Park planetarium. A lecture on the universe concludes with the statement that humans existing by themselves are but a passing episode of little import. At the end of the film, Dean and Mineo discuss the end of the world, and, shortly after, Mineo is killed by the police.

The film does emphasize the toll extracted by delinquent behavior, primarily the tragic deaths of Mineo and of another youth in a car during a "chickie run." However, the blame for such behavior is placed squarely on uncomprehending, unfeeling, and unsympathetic adults and society. Audience sympathy for the youths was also no doubt immeasurably enhanced by the appealing and brilliant performances of the three leads, especially the charismatic James Dean.

Americana: The Institute for the Study of American Popular Culture, www.americanpopularculture.com.

Divided into two sections, this website is dedicated to the analysis of American popular culture. Articles written for a mainstream audience are in the main section, while the second section is devoted to the academic journal *Americana: The Journal of American Popular Culture (1900–Present)*.

Joe Austin and Michael Nevin Willard, eds., *Generations of Youth: Youth Cultures and History in Twentieth-Century America*. New York: New York University Press, 1998.

This collection brings together essays on youth cultures by social historians and American/cultural studies scholars, organized into three sections: "Early Twentieth Century," "War and Postwar," and "Contemporary Youth Culture."

Jane D. Brown, Jeanne R. Steele, and Kim Walsh-Childers, eds., *Sexual Teens, Sexual Media: Investigating Media's Influence on Adolescent Sexuality*. Mahwah, NJ: Lawrence Erlbaum Associates, 2002.

This anthology presents studies sponsored by the Henry J. Kaiser Family Foundation that research the media's role in teen sexuality, gender expectations, sexual orientations, standards of beauty, and relationship norms.

David Buckingham, ed., *Reading Audiences: Young People and the Media*. Manchester: Manchester University Press, 1993.

British scholar Buckingham compiles ten essays that examine young people's use of the popular media in the context of their social activities and experiences.

Thomas Hine, *The Rise and Fall of the American Teenager*. New York: Avon Books, 1999.

Hine investigates the implications of the concept of "teenager" by examining the physiological, psychological, and cultural dimensions of youth; the history of young people from the seventeenth to the twentieth century; and the effects of education and youth culture.

Marsha Kinder, ed., *Kids' Media Culture*. Durham, NC: Duke University Press, 1999.

Bringing together research on the mass media culture of children and adolescents, Kinder divides her anthology into three sections: "Children's Media Culture in the Postwar Era," "Reception and Cultural Identity," and "Pedagogy and Power."

M. Carole Macklin and Les Carlson, eds., *Advertising to Children: Concepts and Controversies*. Thousand Oaks, CA: Sage, 1999.

This book is a compilation of sixteen essays on advertising techniques and the social impact of advertising on children and adolescents. One section goes into depth about cigarette and beer advertising, another section about the Internet and other future directions for research.

Sharon R. Mazzarella and Norma Odom Pecora, eds., *Growing Up Girls: Popular Culture and the Construction of Identity*. New York: Peter Lang, 1999.

Focusing on girls and young women, this anthology examines topics such as Barbie dolls, teen romance novels, girl magazines, feminine hygiene advertising, and all-girl rock bands.

Stephen Miles, *Youth Lifestyles in a Changing World*. Philadelphia: Open University Press, 2000.

Miles argues that it is through lifestyle choices that youth cope with the paradoxes and complexities of life at the beginning of the twenty-first century. He gives special attention to youth and the media, and teenagers as consumers.

Elissa Moses, *The $100 Billion Allowance: Accessing the Global Teen Market*. New York: John Wiley & Sons, 2000.

From a marketing perspective, Moses presents information about teenagers around the world and outlines methods used to win their consumer loyalty.

Claudia Nelson and Lynne Vallone, *The Girl's Own: Cultural Histories of the Anglo-American Girl, 1830–1915*. Athens: University of Georgia Press, 1994.

This collection of eleven essays covers topics such as advice writing for young women, girls in Victorian art and Lewis Carroll's photographs, hygiene and work expectations, and athletic culture in girls' college fiction.

Michael A. Oliker and Walter P. Krolikowski, eds., *Images of Youth: Popular Culture as Educational Ideology*. New York: Peter Lang, 2001.

The twelve essays in this anthology explore the influences of popular culture on teens, predominant representations of youth in popular culture, and images of education in popular culture. The authors examine film, television, music, and sport during the twentieth century to contribute to the history of interaction among adolescents, popular culture, and education.

Grace Palladino, *Teenagers: An American History*. New York: BasicBooks, 1996.

Starting in 1930s, Palladino places American teenagers and their activities in the historical context of each generation in the United States through the 1990s. She covers general trends in music, fashion, film, television, print media, and politics.

Pop Culture Club, www.popcultureclub.org.

This website houses a network of critically acclaimed pop culture sources on the Internet that cover subjects such as television, nostalgia, movies, and music.

Popcultures.com, www.popcultures.com.

Also called "Sarah Zupko's Cultural Studies Center," this website includes sections on journals, archives, articles, theorists and critics, conferences, book reviews, academic programs, publishers, newsgroups and listserves, and general Internet links.

Popular Culture Appreciation Society, http://home.vicnet. net.au/~popcult.

Extensive resources for popular culture research are collected on this website, including a bibliography, a discussion forum, search capabilities, and special sections on pulp fiction and television.

Lucy Rollin, *Twentieth-Century Teen Culture by the Decades*. Westport, CT: Greenwood Press, 1999.

Rollin traces teen culture from 1900 to the 1990s in this reference book that outlines teenage trends related to dating, home life, education, and popular culture, decade by decade.

Victor C. Strasburger, *Adolescents and the Media: Medical and Psychological Impact*. Thousand Oaks, CA: Sage, 1995.

In his research about how adolescents learn from television, Strasburger discusses the impact of violence, sex, drugs, and nutrition on the small screen.

Elliott West, *Growing Up in Twentieth-Century America: A History and Reference Guide*. Westport, CT: Greenwood, 1996.
This book presents a comprehensive history of girlhood and boyhood during the past hundred years in the United States. West gives special attention to the themes of diversity, family economics, and technology.

Whole Pop Magazine Online, www.wholepop.com.
Hosted by "pop culture mavens" Jack Mingo and Erin Barrett, this website offers numerous links to sources covering TV commercials, Pez candies, Legos, retro ads, Star Trek, sports mascots, and much more.

INDEX